Contents

Chapter 1
Browsing

Getting started

The Internet consists of a huge number of computers connected together all over the world. While a small group of connected computers constitutes a network, the Internet is an **Inter**national **Net**work of networks. You can connect to the Internet only at certain points via a phone number that your computer dials into.

This book will tell you how to:

▶ Look up information or go shopping on the Internet

▶ Download pictures, text, music or software

▶ Send and receive e-mail messages

▶ Send large files

The simplest way to look at the Internet is to view web pages with a program called a **Browser**. One of the most common browsers is **Microsoft Internet Explorer** which we shall use in this book.

The browser will not be able to show pages unless the computer is connected to an **Internet Service Provider** or **ISP**. This has probably been done for you already but if not the Appendix explains how to go about it.

To start Internet Explorer:

 ▶ Double-click on the icon for Internet Explorer.

In Windows 98 onwards this is next to the **Start** button.

▶ Otherwise click **Start**, **Programs**, then **Internet Explorer**.

Internet Explorer

▶ A dialogue box may ask if you want to connect. If so, click **Connect**.

A web page will now appear on the screen. This is probably a page that was set as a **default** by your ISP or computer manufacturer.

Tip:
You will hear of other browsers such as **Netscape Navigator** and **Opera**.

Entering an address

You can go to a different page by entering another address.

 Click in the Address box at the top of the screen. The text will be highlighted.

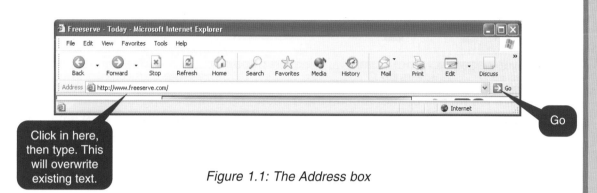

This book uses Internet Explorer versions 6 and 5, which look almost the same. Version 6 looks slightly different in Windows XP.

Go

Click in here, then type. This will overwrite existing text.

Figure 1.1: The Address box

Tip: You could also press the **Enter** key.

 Type in **www.bbc.co.uk** and click on the **Go** button.

This should bring up the BBC web site at the opening or **home** page. It will look similar to the picture below, but not identical since most people and companies are continually changing their web sites.

Click here to scroll down

Figure 1.2: The BBC home page

Web pages may be quite long – like this one. To see the whole page, either click in the scroll bar or press the **Page Down** key.

Tip: If you are looking for something on the page, choose **Find (on This Page)** from the **Edit** menu and enter the word or phrase.

The World Wide Web

This is the best-known part of the Internet, often just called the Web. It consists of hundreds of millions of web pages stored on computers the world over, which you can access from your computer. Most large companies and organisations have a web site and so do more and more private individuals.

Navigating the Web

Most web pages have **hot links** – also called **hypertext** links – which enable you to jump to another page, or back to the top of the same page if it's quite long. When you move the mouse pointer around the screen, the shape changes from an arrow to a hand when it is over a hot area. These are usually text underlined in blue but may also be pictures. When you click on a hot area, the browser jumps to a new page.

 Click on the **History** link in the middle of the page.

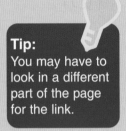
Tip:
You may have to look in a different part of the page for the link.

Tip:
The page may look quite different when you come to look at it but there should still be something of interest.

Figure 1.3: The BBC History page

The History page lets you view the past from many different aspects, and there are numerous other links as well.

 Click on **Timelines** and see what comes up.

4

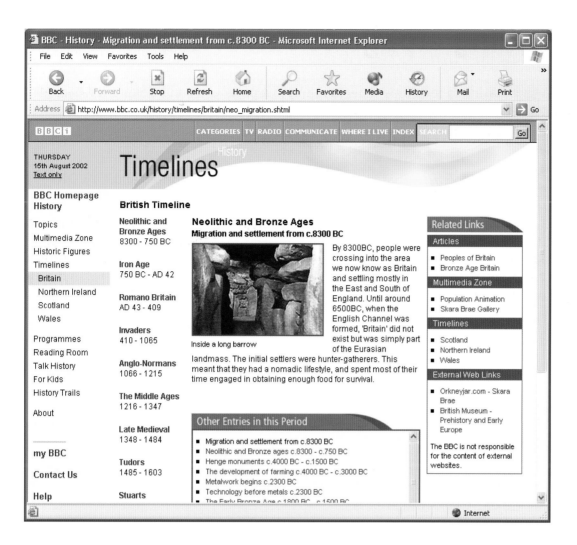

Figure 1.4: History by topic

Returning to a previous page

To go back to the previous page:

▶ Click on the **Back** button at the left of the toolbar. ─────────

▶ Click **Back** repeatedly until you are back at the home page.

Often the links you have already clicked will have changed colour to remind you that you've been there.

▶ Now try clicking the **Forward** button. ─────────

Notice this takes you forward through the pages you were going back through. It is grayed out unless you were going back.

Both buttons have a down-arrow – you can click on it and choose a page from the list.

Tip:
Click some links and see where they lead!

Tip:
You can also use the **Alt** key with the left or right arrow key for **Back** and **Forward**.

Adding a page to Favorites

To save having to remember how to return to a page you can **bookmark** it by adding it to a list of favourite sites.

 Go back to the BBC home page.

 From the menu bar choose **Favorites**, **Add to Favorites** and click **OK**.

Figure 1.5: Adding to Favorites

The web page address

Every web page has a unique address known as the **URL** – for Uniform Resource Locator. This has distinct parts separated by dots, each part having a special significance. A typical address is:

http://www.bbc.co.uk

http:// is the protocol used and stands for **Hypertext Transfer Protocol**, which is the set of rules used by the Internet for sending and receiving data between computers. Some addresses may have **https://** for a secure page with sensitive information, or **ftp://** for file transfer. There's no need to type in **http://** as the browser adds it automatically.

www means World Wide Web and is in most but not all web page addresses.

bbc.co.uk is the **domain name** showing the organisation owning the site and has several parts.

co is the type of site, in this case a commercial organisation. International company domain names generally end in **.com**.

There may also be the name of a file on the end of the address, such as **/index.htm**. web pages are written in a language called **HTML** (for **Hypertext Markup Language**) and each page is a file usually ending in **.htm**.

Here are some sample web addresses – you can probably guess who they belong to. Visit these sites by entering each URL into the **Address** box and clicking on **Go**.

www.disney.com   **www.cam.ac.uk**   **www.worldwildlife.org**

www.nasa.gov   **www.exploratorium.edu**   **www.louvre.fr**

www.museum-london.org.uk

Fact:
Some other codes are **gov** for government, **org** for non-profit organisations, ac for educational sites (**edu** in the USA), or **sch** for schools.
If the site is neither **.com** nor US-based there is usually a country code – **uk** for the UK, **fr** for France, **de** for Germany, **es** for Spain, **ch** for Switzerland, **ie** for Ireland, and so on.
New ones you may see are **biz**, **plc**, **info**, **tv** and **me**.

Note:
You will have heard of **dotcom** companies – this is often misspelt dot.com which would have to be pronounced dot dot com.

A quick way to enter an address

We'll now go back to the BBC home page. Instead of using the **Back** button, here's another way.

 Start typing the address **www.bbc.co.uk**.

Figure 1.6: Selecting an address from a list

Tip:
As soon as you type www.b, a list will appear below as Internet Explorer recognises similar addresses.

▶ Select the address in the list.

Returning to a 'Favorite' page

For a quick way to return to the BBC home page , you could either use the **Back** button again or find it in Favorites where you saved it earlier.

▶ Click the **Favorites** button on the toolbar.

▶ Click the item in the Favorites pane on the left, to bring up that page.

▶ Click the **Favorites** button again to hide the pane.

Figure 1.7

Changing your opening page

It is inconvenient to have Internet Explorer open with a site that is of little interest, particularly if it takes a long time to load. This can be easily changed from the **Options** window. To do this:

 Go to the page you would like to come up, say the BBC home page.

 From the **Tools** menu select **Internet Options**.

 Click **Use Current**.

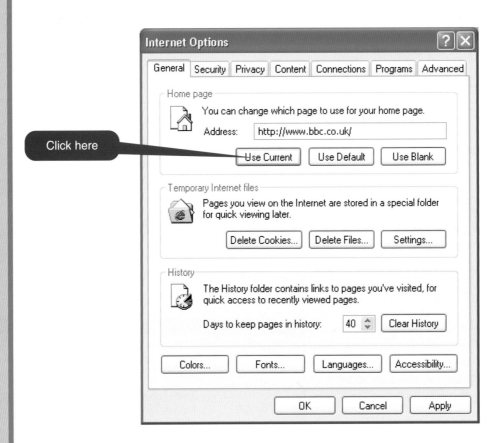

Figure 1.8: Internet Options

There are some other settings on this window that you will meet later.

 Click **OK**.

Ending an Internet session

Unless you have a permanent connection or are on a network, you should disconnect as soon as you have finished since being on the Internet uses your phone line.

While you are connected, the **Dial-up** icon appears in the Status bar at the bottom right of the screen.

▶ Right-click the Dial-up icon and select **Disconnect**.

This disconnects the phone line but does not close Internet Explorer.

▶ Close Internet Explorer by clicking the Close icon (**X**) at the top right of your screen, or by selecting **File**, **Close** from the menu bar.

Note:
Closing Internet Explorer does not automatically disconnect you – you have to instruct the computer to disconnect.

Closing Internet Explorer first

Alternatively you can close Internet Explorer first.

▶ Close Internet Explorer by clicking the Close icon (**X**) at the top right of your screen, or by selecting **File**, **Close** from the menu bar.

A message will appear:

Figure 1.9: Disconnecting

▶ Click **Disconnect Now** to end your connection.

Pop-up advertising

As well as advertisements on a page, at some sites you may be bombarded by new windows suddenly opening on their own with advertising banners. These are a nuisance and there is nothing else to be done but close them ruthlessly as fast as they appear. Don't click on any link or hotspot or you'll be severely held up while yet another unwanted page loads or a program downloads – if this starts to happen click the **Stop** icon on the toolbar.

Other programs

You may find when opening some pages with special graphic or sound effects, that a message asks if you would like to install some program (such as **ShockWave** or **Flash**) that your computer does not have, in order to view the page. It is usually quite safe to do this but the download may take some 20 minutes.

You may also be asked if you wish to download a language **font** (typeface), such as Greek or Chinese. This is not usually necessary.

Other web sites

Some other general interest sites are:

www.nationalgeographic.com	National Geographic
www.discovery.com	Discovery
www.atlapedia.com	Atlapedia – maps and world information
www.open.gov.uk	government information
www.achoo.com	links to health sites
www.vam.ac.uk	Victoria & Albert Museum
www.anagramgenius.com	anagrams galore!
www.howtocleananything.com	
www.anythingleft-handed.co.uk	
www.africam.com	Web cameras

You will find more on **www.payne-gallway.co.uk/internet-rfts**

Chapter 2
Looking Things Up

If you want to look something up but you don't know the address of a suitable web site, there are sites that have links organised by subject matter, sometimes called **Directories** or **Categories**, so that you can browse as in a library. A typical one is **LookSmart**.

 Type **www.looksmart.co.uk** and click **Go**.

 Add the address to **Favorites** so you can return to it later.

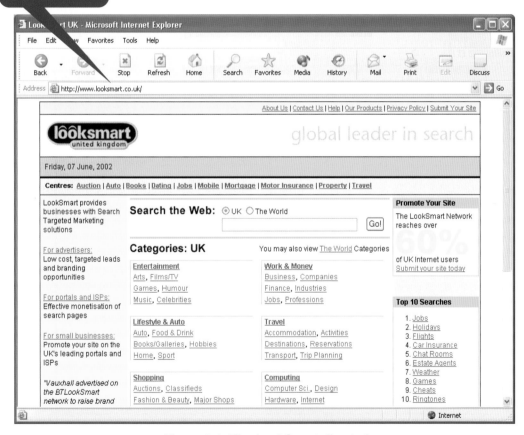

Figure 2.1: The LookSmart directories

LookSmart has a list of main **directories**, each of which when clicked opens a list of subdirectories, and so on.

 For example, if you wanted to find out about **Museums**, scroll down to the **Library** section and click on **Arts & Humanities**, then **Museums & Heritage**.

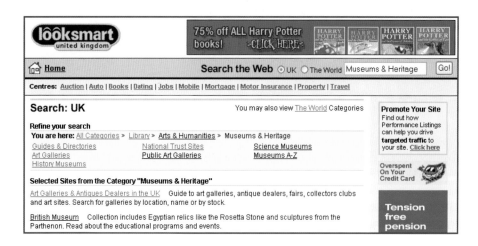

Figure 2.2: Searching through subdirectories

From here you can pick out individual museums.

One of the largest directories is the **Open Directory Project**, which is also used by many other search providers. Compiled by mainly volunteer editors, this aims to build a comprehensive guide to the web.

 Enter **www.dmoz.org** in the address bar and click **Go**.

Figure 2.3: The Open Directory

 Try looking up Chilean wine, acupuncture, whitewater rafting, or whatever is your thing.

Another site worth a look at is **About.com** (**www.about.com**): this is an annotated directory of topics researched and presented by experts.

Some common look-ups

Here are some useful everyday things you might need which can be found in directories, and you will find plenty more.

Making your own UK map

Going somewhere but don't have a map? You can use the LookSmart directory, which you bookmarked earlier.

▶ Click the **Favorites** button on the toolbar.

▶ Select **LookSmart** from the list on the left of the screen.

▶ In the LookSmart directories find **Library**, **Reference Desk**, **Maps**, **UK Maps**.

▶ Click on **Multimap** and add it to **Favorites**.

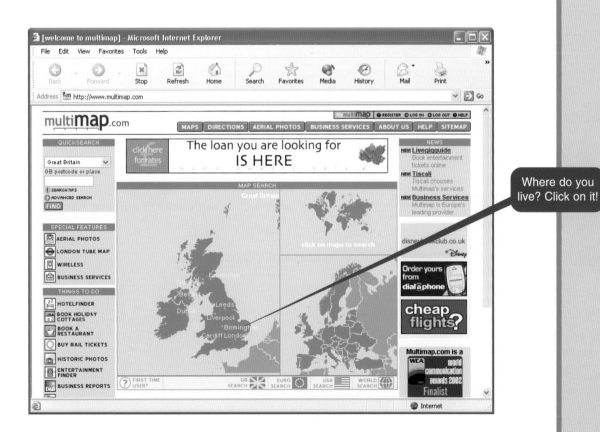

Figure 2.4: Getting a map

This site will draw maps of most of the world at different scales, and down to street level in Europe and USA.

▶ Move the mouse over the UK outline and click on your home area. I've chosen Suffolk.

Figure 2.5: A map of Suffolk

> Click the arrows to centre the map and click the map to zoom in.

To home in accurately on your local area, you can enter a postcode.

> Go back to the home page.

> Enter your home postcode and click **Find**.

Figure 2.6: Finding an area by postcode

You should have a streetmap of your area with a red circle round – or very near – your home!

> Click the **Print** button to print out the page.

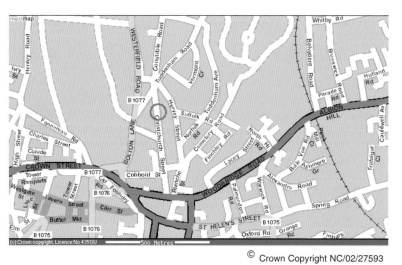

Figure 2.7: A street map

Tip:
Multimap also provides travel directions, aerial photos, and a variety of other services.

Note:
Ordnance Survey copyright allows you one copy for personal use.

Your neighbourhood guide

UpMyStreet gives you lots of information on a locality.

▶ Go to the page **www.upmystreet.com** and enter your postcode.

Figure 2.8: UpMyStreet

When following a link it is sometimes useful to open the page in a separate browser window, without having to click back and forth. To do this, just Shift-click on the link (click while holding **Shift**).

Addresses and phone numbers

With the online Yellow Pages there's no need to visit the library if looking outside your area.

▶ Enter **www.yell.com** and press **Enter**.

▶ Enter the details you are looking for and click **Search**.

Figure 2.9: The Yellow Pages

For directory enquiries, both UK and International, at the cost of a local phone call try **www.192.com** – you may have to register but it's free.

Royal Mail (**www.royalmail.com**) offers postal rates, addresses and postcodes.

General reference

Should your home dictionaries and encyclopedias not be up to the job, **Bartleby** (**www.bartleby.com**) and **Encarta** (**http://encarta.msn.co.uk**) are both free. You'll find others in the **Reference** section in directories.

Figure 2.10: Encarta

Another useful site is **HowStuffWorks** (**www.howstuffworks.com**). This site shows you how almost anything works, often with animations.

Figure 2.11: HowStuffWorks

Reminder: Notice that some addresses have no www.

Tip: If you want to know how your car engine, fridge or CD player works, it's all here.

For music lovers the **All Music Guide** (www.allmusic.com) is a quite exceptional musical encyclopedia.

Tip:
Look up any artist or composer and find full details of styles, biography and recordings.

Figure 2.12: The All Music Guide

For each section – such as Country – there is an introduction, overview of the different styles, essays, "key artists and albums" and new releases. Classical music is no less comprehensive covering periods, genres, and biographies of composers.

The Links bar

Note:
See page 6 for more on Favorites.

As well as having all your preferred sites in the Favorites list, you can also put half a dozen of the sites you use most on the **Links** toolbar, under the Address bar, so as to be in full view.

   Choose **Favorites**, **Add to Favorites**.

   Shorten the name and click on the **Links** folder, then click **OK**.

The Links bar appears either at the right end of the Address bar or below it (if on the right, you can drag it down). If you don't see it, select **View**, **Toolbars**, **Links**.

Tip:
In Internet Explorer 6 click **Create In**.

The Links bar is very versatile – you can drag an address onto it from the Address bar and drag the addresses along to rearrange them. Delete or rename them by right-clicking and choosing from the menu.

Figure 2.13: The Links bar

Looking up people

The Internet is a mine of information when it comes to looking up your ancestry. A good site for this is **www.familytreesearcher.com** which looks up your genealogy in several places on the net.

Figure 2.14: Family Tree Searcher

For the more recent past you can look up all those long-forgotten classmates on **Friends Reunited** (**www.friendsreunited.co.uk**). Just register your details and look up your old school(s) and college, then see who you remember. You can add a picture of yourself – if you're anything like me, no-one would recognise you without one – and even leave a voice recording.

Tip:
Read about images in chapter 7 and e-mail in chapter 9 first before you try this.

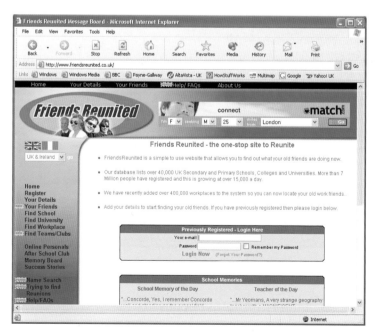

Figure 2.15: Friends Reunited

Chapter 3
Search Engines

Whereas directories are compiled by people and therefore have information that is all relevant to what you are looking up, they may not have some items which are covered somewhere else on the Internet. To track down these elusive details you need something more powerful – a **search engine** – to scour the entire World Wide Web. However, as you will see, you'll discover a whole lot more besides!

Using a search engine

A well-known search engine is **AltaVista**.

Enter the address **www.altavista.co.uk**

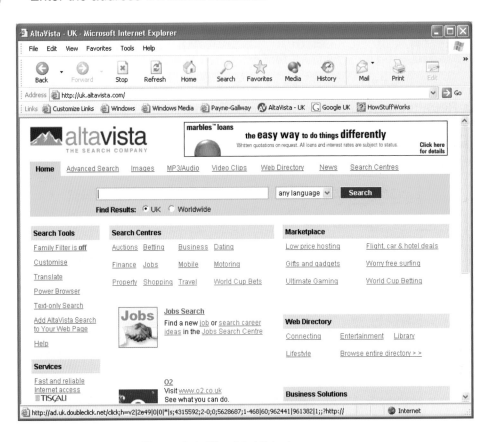

Figure 3.1: The AltaVista home page

This is the UK branch of the US **AltaVista.com**.

Search engines usually have directories, news, local events and information but you can also search by entering a **keyword**.

Searching by keyword

AltaVista allows you to type a word or phrase, and then comes back with a list of related web pages. Suppose you wanted to find out about holiday mobile home rental in France.

 In the search box enter the keywords *mobile home* and click **Search**.

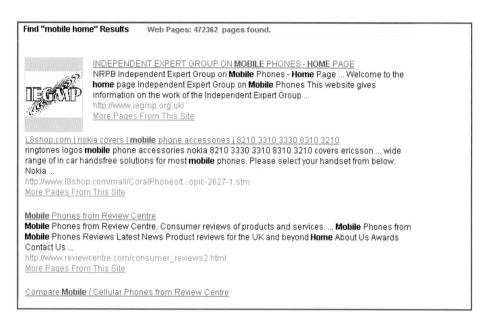

Figure 3.2: AltaVista search results

AltaVista finds a huge number of pages including, in this case, many mobile phone web sites, with some in other languages. Entering *mobile home* was clearly too vague and we need to refine the search.

 In the search box change the keywords to *"Mobile homes"* in quotes, set the language to *English* and click **Search**.

Figure 3.3

This gives far fewer results and cuts out all mention of mobile phones by looking for a phrase.

 Have a look at some of the references by clicking on the links.

The results are shown, 10 to a page, with the most relevant first. Scroll down to see subsequent pages.

Results Pages: 1 2 3 4 5 6 7 8 9 10 Next >>

Figure 3.4

Including and excluding pages

There are still too many sites that are not directly relevant since we are not interested in UK. We can tell AltaVista to exclude these by adding a keyword with a minus in front. Similarly, if we are particularly interested in a topic – such as rental and France – we can add keywords with a plus in front.

 Try adding *–UK +rental +France*

Figure 3.5

This will cut down the results considerably, and you can refine it still further with more keywords. Selecting **Worldwide** will find more sites but many will be partly in French.

It is sometimes convenient to save your results page to refer to later.

 From the **File** menu choose **Save As** and find a suitable folder on your computer to put it in.

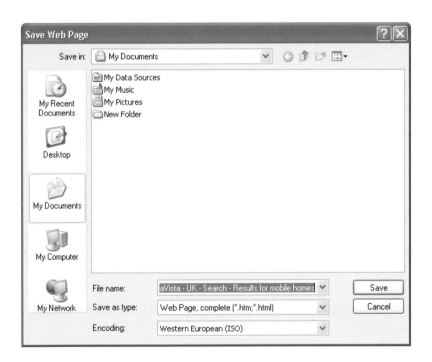

Figure 3.6

Missing page

You may find that your browser cannot find a page although you clicked on a link to it, and it displays something like this.

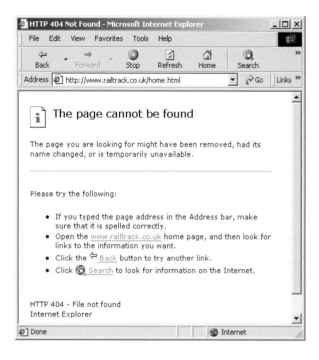

Figure 3.7: A missing page

Tip:
You'll see a similar message if you type an address in wrongly and the browser can't find it.

Don't worry, this often happens! The Internet is growing so fast that many web pages have mistakes in their link addresses. This may be because the page that a link points to has been removed or had its address changed.

Search engines v Directories

Directories, as we have seen, are compiled by people and so contain only information that is relevant to each category. They are unlikely to have anything obscure – like that owl-hooting contest you might have wanted to look up. Search engines on the other hand seem to go off into the ether and come back with a truly impressive number of searched pages even though a large number of these are irrelevant. What's going on here? Has it really gone round the world while you sharpened your pencil?

In fact, search engines keep an index of keywords which is continually added to by special programs – known as **crawlers**, **spiders** or **bots** – which continually run all over the web (taking several months) collecting keywords from each web site. These embedded keywords (called **meta tags**), invisible in normal view, are put on the site by the designer so as to be found by crawlers and cause the site to pop up on search results pages as often as possible. With vague or misleading keywords a page will often appear unexpectedly.

Fact:
A few engines index the whole site.

Google

One of the best known and most powerful search engines is **Google**.

 Enter the address **www.google.com**.

Figure 3.8: Google

 Add it to Favorites.

Google has a more uncluttered home page but also has directories and images. It generally finds more relevant results than other search engines.

Suppose you wanted to find the Prime Minister's official web site.

 Type *10 Downing Street* into the search box and click the **Google Search** button.

Google comes back with a list of links to **www.number-10.gov.uk** of which the home page is at the top.

Figure 3.9: The Google results page

Click the first link to admire the Number 10 site.

The Google results are consistently so relevant that they provide an alternative button **I'm Feeling Lucky** which takes you straight to the first result without seeing the list.

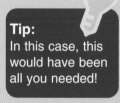

Figure 3.10: The Number 10 site

 Go back to the Google home page.

Time for another search. Suppose we wanted a cooking recipe for salsa.

 In the search box, enter *salsa* and click **Google Search**.

Figure 3.11

This finds a huge number of references but mostly for dance, music or cycles! Some are not in English.

Figure 3.12

We need to refine the search by including sauces and recipes and excluding music, dance and cycles. We could do this using + and – as before or we could use the Advanced Search window.

Advanced search

 Click the **Advanced Search** link next to the search box. (See Figure 3.12)

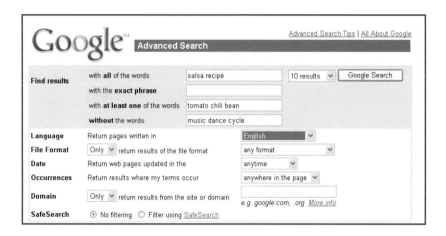

Figure 3.13 Google Advanced Search window

 Fill in the boxes as shown above.

The line **tomato chili bean** you could also have typed in the general search box as *tomato OR chili OR bean* (the **OR** must be in capitals).

 Click **Google Search**.

Figure 3.14

This will give a much more concentrated set of results to browse through.

When following a link from the results page this often leads to several further links and may still be a false trail, by which time you need to press **Back** repeatedly to return to the results page; or you may even find the Back button is grayed out. It is best to open the link in a new browser window which you can close when no longer needed. To do this, just **Shift-click** on the link.

Tip:
The **Language** box lets you specify pages in English only.

Further refinements

The Advanced Search window shown above also has a few other options such as returning recent pages only. Google normally searches for keywords anywhere in the page but you can restrict this to the title (hidden text set by the web site designer), text or URL (the page address), or in links to the page.

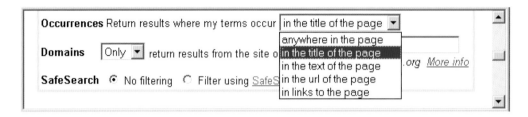

Figure 3.15

Instead of opening the dialogue, you can also specify these directly in the search line with special 'modifiers'. For example, **inurl:Amazon** or **intitle:Amazon** will find only sites with *Amazon* in the address or the title respectively. You will find full information on the Search Help pages.

Some search engines (AltaVista but not Google) allow 'wildcards' to cater for variations in words. Thus *compan** will find **company**, **companies**, **companion**, etc.

 Add **Google** and **AltaVista** to your **Links** bar.

For more UK-oriented results there's also **www.google.co.uk**.

Relevance of the results

Some search engines consistently find more relevant results than others. Most go on the number of keyword tags they find in a particular site, but Google – currently the leader of the pack – also sets the priority by the number of other sites referring to that site.

Other search engines

There are numerous other search engines, with more appearing constantly. Worth mentioning are **Yahoo**, and **AskJeeves**.

Yahoo has a UK site **www.yahoo.co.uk** with extensive directories.

Figure 3.16: Yahoo

Tip:
You can search either worldwide, UK only or Ireland only.

FACT

Fact:
This is a good example of a portal site – where you go to find links to lots of other sites.

For simple straightforward queries, **Ask Jeeves** (**www.ask.co.uk**) understands natural language – that is, plain English.

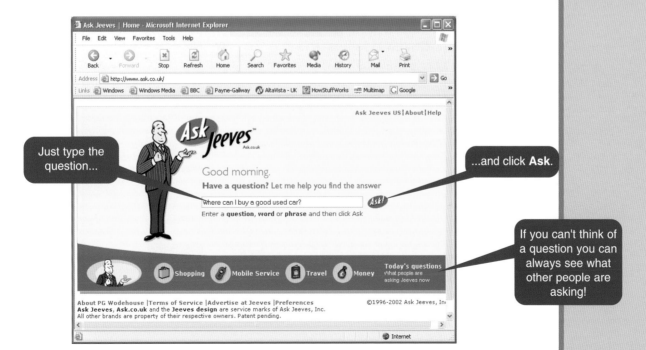

Figure 3.17: Ask Jeeves

Rather than reply instantly, Jeeves presents you with related questions (hand-compiled) using dropdown menus which will hopefully lead you to the answer, and you'll probably find other interesting things along the way.

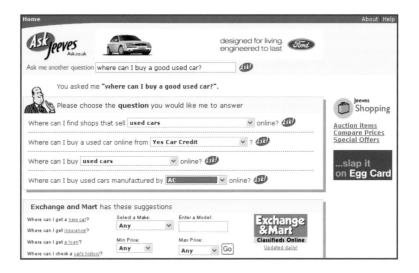

Figure 3.18: Ask Jeeves results

Whatever the query, whether used cars or train times, Jeeves is immediately on the case with a list of helpful suggestions.

Metasearch engines

A few search engines pass on the query to several others. In **MetaCrawler** (**www.metacrawler.com**) you can select from other engines or directories and view the results by relevance, site or source.

Figure 3.19: MetaCrawler

Metor (**www.metor.com**) is similar but also offers specific searches from sites specialising in each topic.

Figure 3.20: Metor

Metasearches take longer than searching just one engine so you can set a time-out.

Other searches

Aside from information, search engines let you search for images, video clips, sounds, and other types of file such as documents, spreadsheets and pdf (Portable Document Format) files. We'll look at these later.

Yet another alternative is to download the search engine program **Copernic** from **www.copernic.com**.

Even this hasn't exhausted search engines! You'll find updates on

www.payne-gallway.co.uk/internet-rfts

Tip:
Some engines are specialised, such as FindArticles (**www.findarticles.com**) for magazines.

You can do a lot of work without even logging on to the Internet, using pages that you have visited on previous occasions. This avoids tying up the phone line and cuts down on the phone bills!

 Open **Internet Explorer** either by double-clicking the icon or choosing **Start, Programs, Internet Explorer**.

You may see a dialogue box similar to the one below. If so, click **Work Offline**.

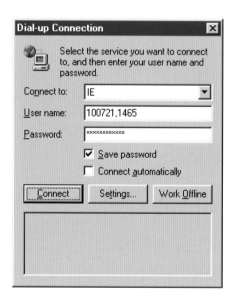

Figure 4.1: Choosing to work offline

If **Connect Automatically** has been checked in this dialogue box, it will not appear next time and you will be automatically connected.

 In that case, right-click the **Dial-up** icon in the bar at the bottom right of your screen and select **Disconnect**.

You are now working offline.

Tip:
Selecting **Work Offline** from the **File** menu will not automatically disconnect you! This makes Internet Explorer start up without connecting.

The Favorites List

The **Favorites** list is very useful when you are working on a project. You will often find you need to go back to pages you have visited previously. Sometimes you will want to delete items from the **Favorites** list or reorganise it so that the most used sites are near the top of the list.

In **Internet Explorer**, click **Favorites** on the toolbar. Notice the **Favorites** list pane opens on the left.

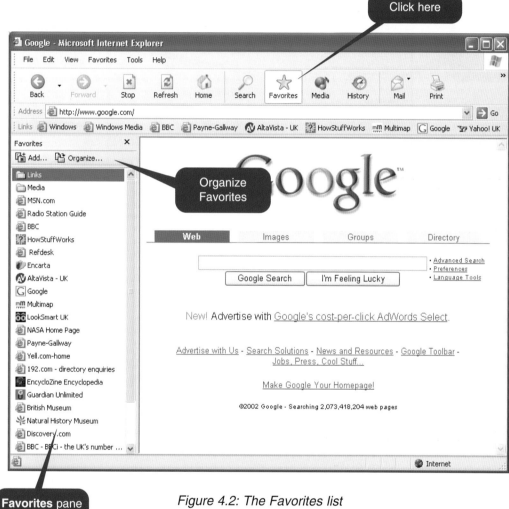

Figure 4.2: The Favorites list

You can ignore some of the ones at the top which may be to do with your Internet provider, and you may also have **My Documents** which is where Windows puts your **Word** files. You can now choose a web page from the list.

Organising the Favorites list

Tip:
You can select **Organize Favorites** from the **Favorites** menu.

The entries in the **Favorites** list appear in the order that they were added. You may want to change the order, perhaps moving the most useful ones up to the top.

 Click on **Organize Favorites** (see Figure 4.2).

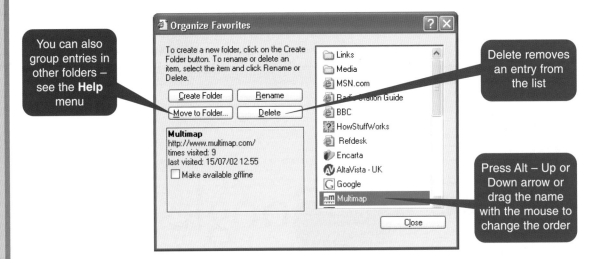

You can also group entries in other folders – see the **Help** menu

Delete removes an entry from the list

Press Alt – Up or Down arrow or drag the name with the mouse to change the order

Figure 4.3: The Organize Favorites window

The **Organize Favorites** window lets you move entries around. For example, to move **Multimap** up:

 Select **Multimap** in the list.

 Hold down the **Alt** key and press the **Up** arrow. Alternatively you can hold down the mouse button and drag it up the list – a solid line shows where you can drop it.

Some of the entries may have rather long names. You can use the **Rename** button to shorten them.

Similarly, you can move items down, delete them or move them to another folder. If you double-click on the **Links** folder you will see the items which appear on the **Links** toolbar.

Note:
Deselecting is the opposite of selecting.

 Click the **Close** button.

 You can hide the **Favorites** window by clicking the **Favorites** button on the toolbar to deselect it.

The History list

Internet Explorer keeps track of all the pages you have visited and when. This is kept in the **History** list.

▶ Click on the **History** icon in the toolbar and notice the **History** list pane opens on the left.

▶ Click the arrow next to **View** and select **By Date**.

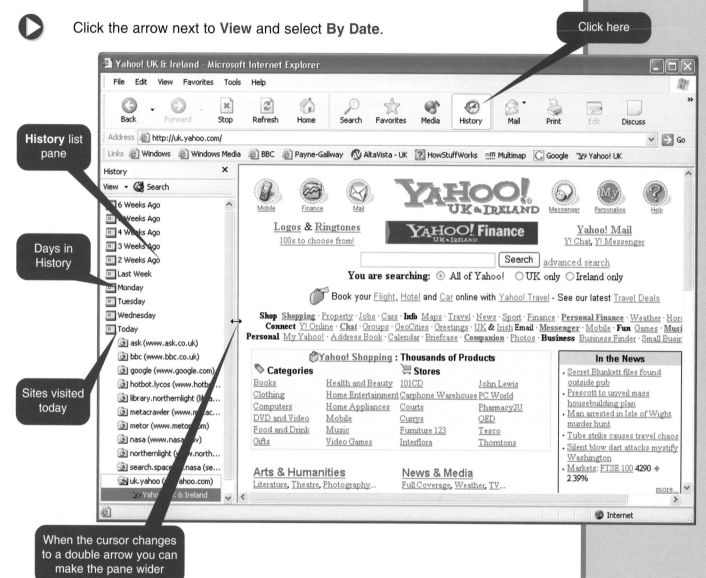

Figure 4.4: The History list pane

If the **History** pane needs to be widened:

▶ Place the cursor over the right border until it changes to a double arrow.

▶ Click and drag it halfway across the window.

In the list, the pages visited are grouped by day, ending in **Today**. Clicking on an icon expands or contracts it.

▶ Click on the icon for **Today** to expand it, if not already expanded.

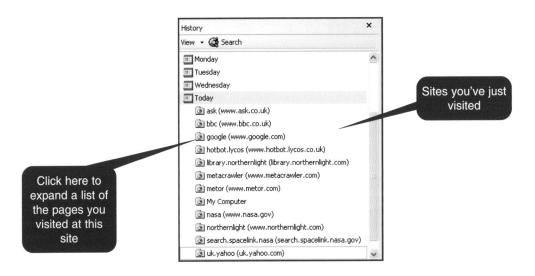

Sites you've just visited

Click here to expand a list of the pages you visited at this site

Figure 4.5: The History list

A recent site you visited was **www.google.com.**

 Click on the name.

The list now shows all the pages visited on that site.

Figure 4.6: Expanding the History list

 Open some of the other days and see where you – or someone else – has been browsing lately.

As well as viewing the **History** list by day, you can also order it by **Site** or by **Most Visited**.

 Click the **View** button and choose **By Site**.

Click here

Figure 4.7: The History list ordered by site

If you can't find the site you're looking for, you can always search.

 Click the **Search** button next to **View**, enter a name and click **Search Now**.

 Click on **View** again when you've finished searching

Figure 4.8: Searching for a site

This will list all the occurrences.

 To close the **History** list, click on **History** on the toolbar. ———

Note:
As well as web sites, this will also list recently-used files and folders on your computer, which can be confusing.

Browsing Offline

When your browser is not connected to the Internet you will find that you can still see some pages you visited most recently. This is because **Internet Explorer** stores these pages on disk, in what is known as **cache**. They are only held for as long as the pages are kept in **History**.

Figure 4.9: The Title bar tells you that you are working offline

Internet Explorer tells you in the title bar if it's displaying a page offline. And you may also notice a news item looks rather old!

While offline, if you click on a link to a page that is not saved, you'll be prompted to connect again.

Figure 4.10: You will need to connect to go to a page that has not been saved

Refreshing a page

If you get a message that a web page cannot be displayed, or you are not sure if you are looking at the latest version of the page, click the **Refresh** button (or you can press the F5 key on your keyboard).

If a page you are trying to look at is taking too long to open (the mouse pointer keeps showing an hour-glass), click the **Stop** button. This often happens if a page has a lot of pictures.

Tip:
You can make a page always available offline from the **Organize Favorites** window (see Figure 4.3).

Tip:
You can tell if a page is not saved. When you pass the cursor over it, there is a black circle next to the hand.

Reviewing the History list

Suppose you are looking up recipes. You could look in the **History** list for a salsa page you found in the last chapter.

▶ In the **History** window, click on **View** then **By Site**.

▶ Click on a **Google** icon to show the pages visited.

Figure 4.11: Selecting a page from the History list

From here you can find a suitable site and open it.

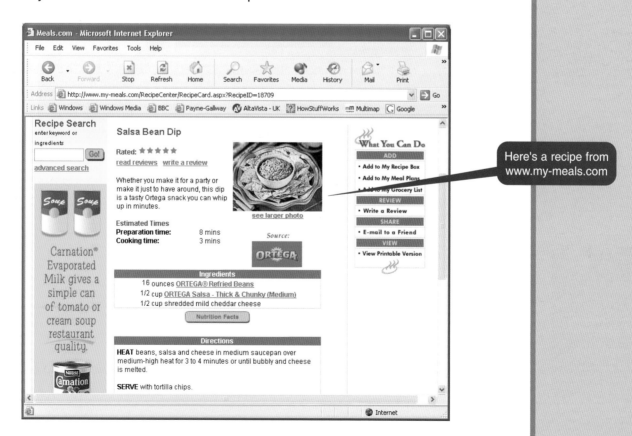

Figure 4.12: Revisiting a page in the History list

Copying text

Suppose you want to copy some of the text and graphics from this web site into a **Word** document.

▶ Make sure you have **Word** running and if you don't have a blank document open choose **File**, **New**.

▶ Go back to **Internet Explorer** (press **Alt-Tab** or select it from the bar at the bottom of the screen).

▶ Drag to select a few lines of text.

▶ From the **Edit** menu, choose **Copy**.

▶ Go back to **Word** and from the **Edit** menu, choose **Paste**.

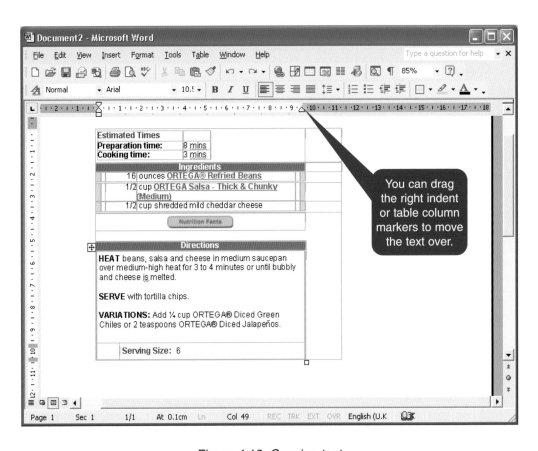

Figure 4.13: Copying text

The text is copied into **Word** as a table. It is probably more convenient to copy the individual pieces of text into another document.

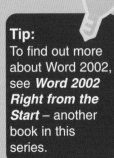

Note:
If the area you selected contained an image, this will also appear in your Word document. However, in this case the image is only a link to the web page and will disappear when you go offline.

Copying graphics

In this case, the picture was part of a table on the web page and copied over with the text, but sometimes you have to copy the graphics separately.

    In **Internet Explorer**, right-click on the picture you want to copy and select **Copy**.

    Go back to the Word document, right-click on the document and select **Paste**.

The Image toolbar

In Internet Explorer 6 when you hover the mouse over an image, a toolbar should appear which allows you to save, print or e-mail the image.

Tip:
In **Word**, you'll need to set **Wrapping** or **Layout** to get the picture alongside the text. Right-click the picture and choose **Format Picture**.

Updating offline pages

When visiting a page offline, you will only see it as it was when last open online. You can arrange for pages you frequently want to look at to be updated automatically when you are online. To do this:

 Find the pages in the Organize Favorites window and for each check the **Make Available Offline** box.

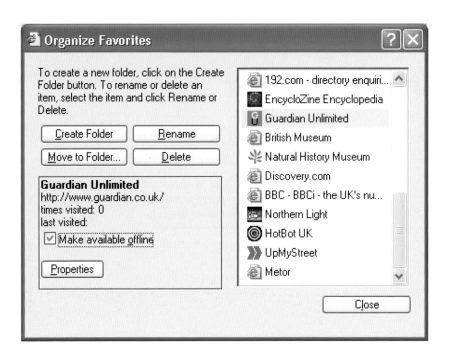

Figure 4.14: Making a page available offline

Internet Explorer will save the current version of each page to view offline. Another time, when you want to update some or all of these pages to the current versions:

 Select **Tools**, **Synchronize** and check the box next to each page you want to update.

If you want Internet Explorer to start up in offline mode without connecting, select **File**, **Work Offline**.

Saving pages

Instead of recalling a page offline as above, you can also save it as a file, either complete with pictures or text only, using **File**, **Save As**.

Chapter 5
Downloading Files

You can download pictures, video clips, sounds and software from the Internet. In this chapter you will learn how to download and save pictures, sounds and software.

You'll need to keep them in separate folders where they can easily be found again when you need them. If you don't know how to make a new folder, here's how.

Creating a new folder

▶ In Windows Explorer select the **My Documents** folder.

▶ Choose **File**, **New**, **Folder**.

Tip:
To open **Windows Explorer** right-click the **Start** button and choose **Explorer**.

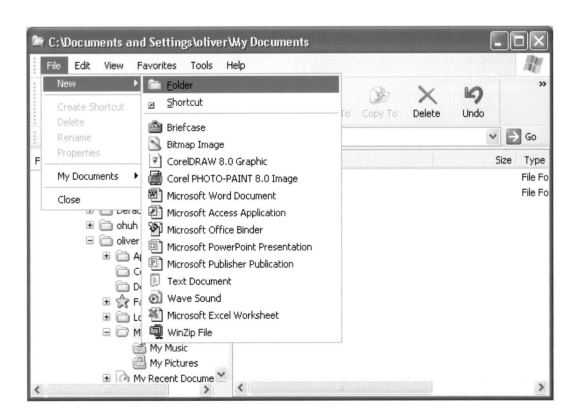

Figure 5.1: Making a new folder

Tip:
To find out more about files and folders, see *Computers Right from the Start* – another book in this series.

A new folder appears in the right-hand pane.

Figure 5.2: Naming a new folder

▶ Type **Pictures** to rename it, then click away from it.

Looking for pictures

The Internet has lots of pictures you can download. Some are copyright but many are free. Let's find something brightly coloured, say a kingfisher.

▶ Open **Internet Explorer** and connect to the Internet.

▶ Open the **Favorites** list and choose **AltaVista**.

▶ Click on **Images**.

You can choose several types of image from UK or worldwide. Suppose we wanted to see colour photos of birds.

Figure 5.3: Searching for a picture of a kingfisher

▶ Fill in the details as shown above and click **Search**.

AltaVista returns a few hundred images. Many of them are are not free to copy – a popup message may warn you of this when you run the mouse pointer over them, otherwise clicking on an image will give further details.

▶ Find a suitable image.

This is the number of 'picture elements' or pixels

Most images are **.jpg** or **.gif**

11398091.jpg
256x170 8 KB

This is the file size of this 'thumbnail' image

Figure 5.4: Selecting a picture

▶ To copy the picture, right-click it and choose **Save Picture As**.

▶ Give the picture a name and save the file in the folder you created, or another suitable one.

▶ You can try clicking the picture to see it at a larger size.

If you don't like these, check the next **Results** pages. You can also enter *royalty-free* as a search keyword!

Save a few images into your Pictures folder. You can also search for images on the Web at **Google** using the image search tab.

Using a downloaded graphic

You can now open the file in a graphics package, or put it in a **Word** document (using **Insert**, **Picture**, **From File**).

Picture files on web pages are usually stored in either **.jpg** or **.gif** format since these are compressed, giving small files which are quick to load.

Note:
Images from **Corbis** (www.corbis.com) are free to copy if they are watermarked and some are also royalty-free. Check on the site.

Tip:
Once you've saved a lot of image files, a graphic viewer program is useful to browse them. We'll be looking at one later in this chapter.

Fact:
.jpg and **.gif** files lose some quality in the compression process so are not very high resolution – a bit 'dotty' like a newspaper photograph.

Downloading sounds

AltaVista offers sounds and music in different formats. For some files, Windows may prompt you to download special software.

▶ Still in AltaVista, select **MP3/Audio** and click **Search** to see what comes up.

Figure 5.5: Selecting a sound

▶ Have a look at some results. I've found Ralph Duren's bird calls.

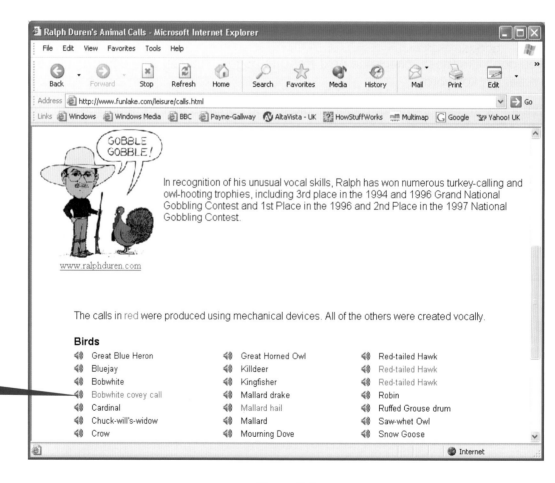

Click here to hear it

Figure 5.6

Sounds can be played using **Windows Media Player**. In Internet Explorer 6 you can press the **Media** button to open it as a pane in the Internet Explorer screen.

▶ Click the **Media** button if you have it, then click on the sound file.

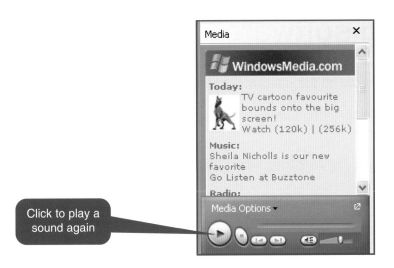

Click to play a sound again

Figure 5.7: Playing a sound in the Media pane

You can copy the file by right-clicking on the icon and choosing **Save Target As**, which will prompt you for which folder to put it in. You can also brighten up your letters by putting a sound file into, for example, a Word document and e-mailing it.

 Right-click the icon and choose **Copy**, then right-click in the document and choose **Paste**.

Figure 5.8: A sound file in a document

Windows Media Player will play all types of sound files, including music compressed as MP3. Some links simply play a sound file without downloading it – a process known as **streaming**. Many sites offer streamed music.

Video clips

These are available in several formats

Figure 5.9: Selecting a video

You may be prompted to download special software such as **RealPlayer** or **Quicktime**. Files tend to be large and the effect can be jerky without a fast machine. Video can also be streamed.

Downloading software

There's a lot of software available on the Internet and a good site is **Tucows**.

 In the **Address** box enter http://tucows.blueyonder.co.uk and click **Go**.

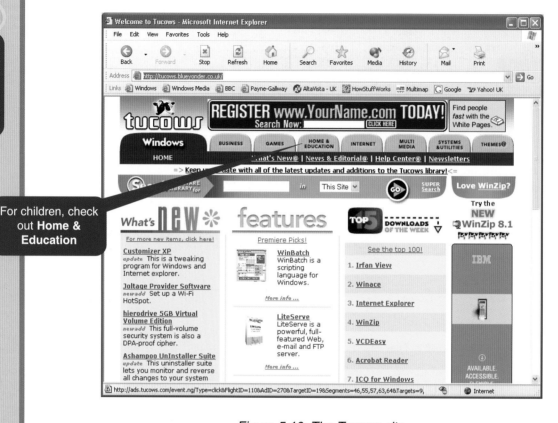

Figure 5.10: The Tucows site

Programs are either for sale, **shareware** (you try before you buy), **freeware** or demonstrations (both free). Software for Windows is arranged by category. We are going to download some freeware – an image viewer to look at your pictures!

 First make a new folder called **Download** as in Figure 5.1.

 Click the **Multimedia** tab, look for **Image Viewers** and scroll down the list to **IrfanView**.

You will see something like this. Programs have a 'cow rating'– from 1 to 5!

The file size

Irfan View 3.75	July 14th, 2002	Freeware	808.0K	Windows 95/98
This feature-rich image viewer and converter supports many formats.				Windows Me
				Windows NT
				Windows 2000
				Windows XP

Figure 5.11

 Click the appropriate link on the right for your version of Windows.

A dialogue box asks whether you want to open it or save it.

Figure 5.12

▶ Choose **Save**. In the Save As dialogue box, go to your **Download** folder then click **Save**.

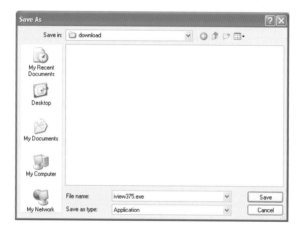

Figure 5.13

The file downloads, taking about 3 minutes with the average phone connection.

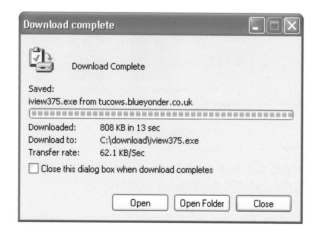

Figure 5.14

▶ Once complete, click **Open Folder** to show the downloaded file in your folder.

The program can now be installed.

▶ Double-click the file in the folder and the install screen should appear.

Tip:
To see how the download is going using a modem, hold the mouse pointer over the **Dial-up** icon. A status message pops up.

Warning:
Check the size of the file is about 800Kb; if not the download may have broken off. If nothing happens when you double-click the file, try downloading again.

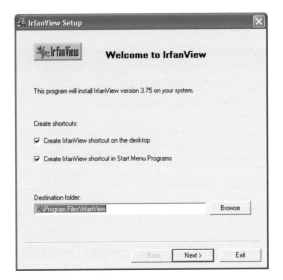

Figure 5.15

Tip:
Or double-click the icon on the desktop.

 Without changing any settings, click **Next** on each screen, then **Done**.

The program is now installed. To run it:

 Click **Start**, **Programs**, **IrfanView** and find the program.

 Choose **File**, **Thumbnails** and find your **Pictures** folder.

Figure 5.16

 In the right-hand window choose **Options**, **Select All** then **File**, **Start Slideshow** and watch the pictures flashing up!

While **Windows 2000** and **XP** also offer thumbnails and slideshow, with IrfanView you can actually change the images, cropping off bits you don't want, adjusting colour and contrast, and removing red-eye or mother-in-law from photos.

This is particularly useful for tidying up pictures you have taken on a scanner or digital camera – for more on these topics, see **Computers Right from the Start** in this series.

Take a look at the **Help** menu to see all the different things you can do.

Download managers

When downloading a large file, you cannot do anything else in the meantime and if the connection breaks you then have to start again. Using a **download manager** such as **GetRight** (www.getright.com) not only lets you interrupt the download but automatically resumes if the connection breaks.

Executable files

When you download a program file, it will have a name ending in **.exe** meaning it is an **executable** file. The program may install itself and start running automatically. Some **.exe** files are not the program file itself but a compressed or **zipped** version shrunk for faster downloading. The file is self-extracting. To expand or **unzip** it:

▶ Make a new folder as in Figure 5.1.

▶ Find the file and copy it into the folder.

▶ Double-click on the file, **Browse** to the target folder then **Unzip**.

The original and much larger file will now be in the folder. If it too is a **.exe** file, double-click on it to install or run the program.

Reading .pdf files

Sometimes documents you download have names ending in .pdf – for **Portable Document Format**. To read them, you need a program called **Acrobat Reader**. If it's not on your machine you can download it free from www.adobe.com

Viruses

There is a risk that a file you download (or copy from a floppy disk) could be infected with a virus – a piece of computer code that can have various effects ranging from mischief to damaging your computer. Make sure you have a **Virus Checker** program installed to catch the viruses as they arrive.

Tip:
Hold down the **Ctrl** key and drag the file to copy it.

Tip:
Once **Acrobat Reader** is installed on your computer, you just double-click a **.pdf** file in **Windows Explorer** to open it.

Tip:
If you are on a network, it should already be protected.

Peer-to-peer networks

Music and other files to download are available not only from conventional web sites where you download from a server, but also via **peer-to-peer** networks (**P2P**). Conventionally the Internet is **client-server** where you (the client) download from a web site (the server). However, a recent and controversial development lets you communicate and share files directly with thousands of other users and vice versa. With software downloaded from a site such as **BearShare** (**www.bearshare.com**) you can set up your folders of files you want to share with others on the network and search their folders for files that you want. The file exchange uses a protocol called **Gnutella** and the network is termed a Gnutella-net. There are legal implications to the sharing of files, particularly music but, notwithstanding, this new Internet phenomenon looks set to grow.

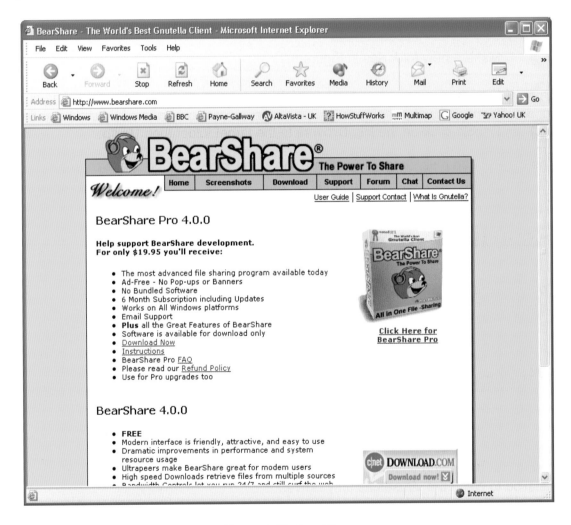

Figure 5.17: BearShare

Other software sites

Other sites are **http://download.cnet.com/** and **http://shareware.cnet.com** and you will find more on **www.payne-gallway.co.uk/internet-rfts**

Chapter 6
Shopping and Services

You can use the Internet for buying numerous things and it's also an invaluable consumer guide. You pay by credit card but provided that you enter the payment details on a secure site – with an address beginning **https://** – it's as safe as the high street. Let's take a look.

The weekly food shop

One of the most developed online sites is **Tesco's**. There's the impressive range of foodstuffs and you can order videos, books, electrical goods, home furnishings and baby stuff. You can even arrange your personal finances (mortgage, insurance, ISAs, credit cards, loans, …), order currencies if you're travelling and have flowers delivered.

 Go to the site **www.tesco.com**

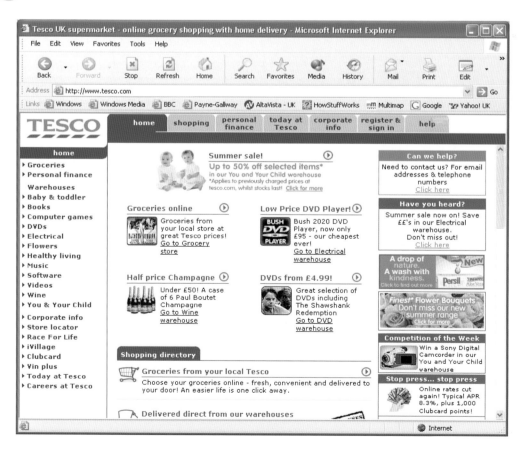

Figure 6.1: The Tesco site

Click on the **register & sign in** tab.

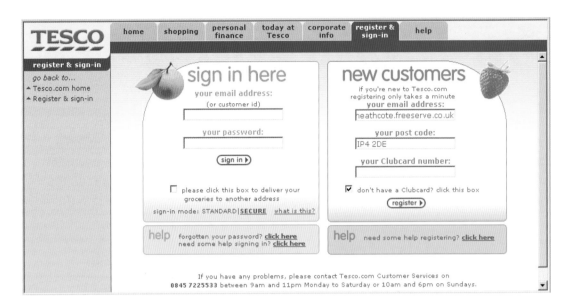

Figure 6.2

 Enter your e-mail address and post code, click **register** and give yourself a password.

You are immediately given a clubcard number – keep this handy with your password and proceed to the online grocery. Here you just browse the list, enter the quantities and click **Add to Basket**.

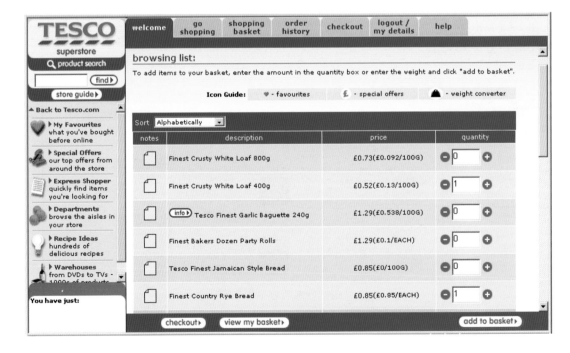

Figure 6.3: Choosing groceries

 You can look at other sections from the Store Guide on the left, view your basket so far and change any quantities.

Figure 6.4

▶ Having chosen what you need from all sections, you now click on **Checkout**, book a delivery slot then enter your card details on a secure page.

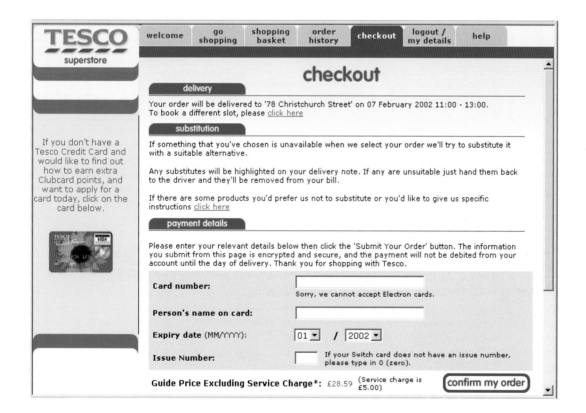

Figure 6.5: Checkout

And that's all there is to it!

House buying

Fish4 Homes offers a handy search tool for finding properties throughout the UK, both for buying or renting.

 Go to **www.fish4.co.uk/homes**

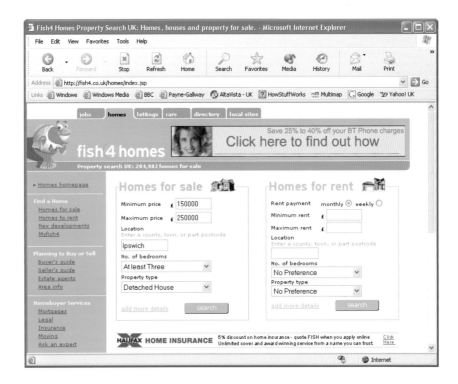

Figure 6.6: Fish4 Homes

 Assuming you are looking to buy rather than rent, enter your price range, location, number of bedrooms and type of property as above and click **Search**.

You then further specify new or older house, number of reception and bathrooms, garden and parking availability. The site now queries thousands of properties and lists the results by price, location or property type.

Figure 6.7: House search results

You can now click to see more details on a house, contact the Estate Agent and arrange to view.

Figure 6.8

Also available are Homebuyer Services with help on legal fees, insurance, moving and mortgages.

 Click **Calculate** to see the monthly mortgage payments.

Figure 6.9: Working out the mortgage payments

You could also check out the locality for subsidence, pollution, flooding and other risks on **www.home-envirosearch.com**.

DIY

Should your house need a few odd jobs doing on it why not check out the **B&Q** site at **www.diy.com** which has all you need.

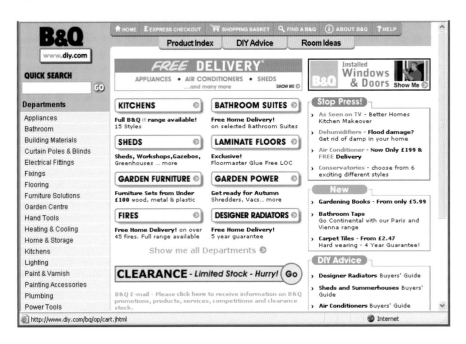

Figure 6.10: B&Q

Decoration

On the **Dulux** site **www.dulux.co.uk** there is the full range of paints as expected.

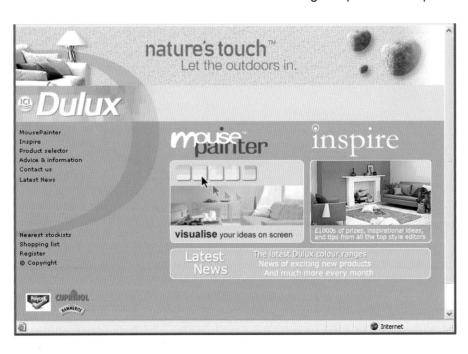

Figure 6.11: The Dulux site

Amazon

If it's books you're after, using an online store like Amazon is simple, the choice is extensive and it can be cheap. There are also DVDs, music, videos and more.

 Go to **www.amazon.co.uk** and click on the **Books** tab.

Figure 6.12: The Amazon site

You can browse by the book categories on the left or search for a book by author, title or ISBN.

The most popular titles can attract up to 50% discount. Having made your choice, you add it to your shopping basket and head for the checkout.

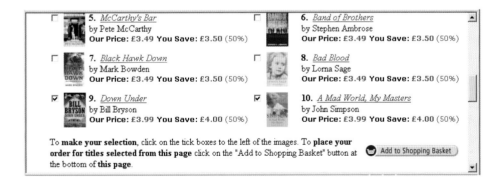

Figure 6.13: Choosing books

There is also gift-wrapping and vouchers to take some of the hassle out of shopping for presents. Christmas shopping in particular is greatly simplified by Amazon's multi-address deliveries – you can enter a separate delivery address and gift tag information for each item in your shopping basket.

Banking

The '90s were all about telephone banking, but the Internet has opened up new avenues and most High Street banks offer online services. This is **Lloyds TSB** (**www.lloydstsb.com**) which offers most banking services via your computer.

Figure 6.14: Internet banking

The first virtual bank is **Smile** from the Co-operative Bank. It is a genuine online bank with no expensive branch network to maintain so can offer higher interest rates.

You can open a Smile account online and it will generate downloadable letters to transfer your existing banking business over, closing the old account and transferring salary or any other incoming payments to the new account, as well as direct debits and standing orders.

Go to **www.smile.co.uk**

Figure 6.15: Internet banking with Smile

Getting online

Once your bank account is running, it's as easy as connecting to the Internet. By accessing your account online using encrypted security codes, you can pay bills, set up, amend and cancel standing orders and direct debits, and transfer money to other Smile accounts, or to accounts anywhere in the world (this takes up to five banking days).

Using Smile's services

Paying for goods and services is easy – you can use the Smile chequebook and guarantee card, or the Visa debit card. For cash, however, it's back to traditional methods, from Link and Visa cash machines, High Street banks using the Visa debit card (some banks may charge for this), writing a cheque at a post office or using supermarkets' cashback facilities.

Cash deposits can be paid into your account via a post office or bank, using a credit slip (banks may charge for this). Cheques can be paid in the same way, or by post to Smile's HQ.

Finance

Moneyworld (www.moneyworld.co.uk) gives borrowing and savings rates, life insurance, share prices and tax information, as well as an excellent section on the performance of all the FTSE shares, unit and investment trusts, pension funds, pep's etc.

Figure 6.16: Financial help from Moneyworld

Comparing utility charges

Buy (www.buy.co.uk) lets you enter the details of your current supplier, payment method and annual usage. For electricity it requests this in £.

Use the 'dual fuel' calculator if you're using one supplier for both gas and electricity.

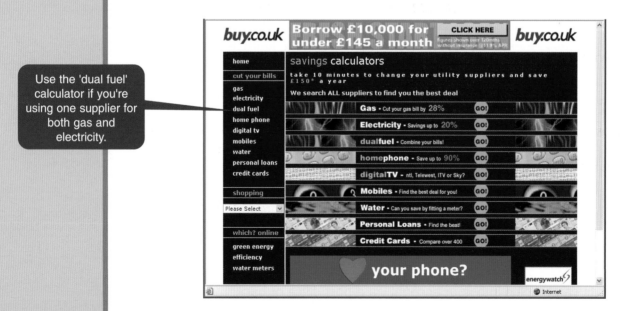

Figure 6.17: Comparing utility charges

For both electricity and gas, it returns the top three best buys. There is an option for comparing your annual water company charge with the forecast metered costs.

Auctions

Online auctions are very popular and one of the most widely used is **Ebay**.

 Go to **www.ebay.co.uk**

Figure 6.18: Ebay

Here you can browse what's on offer from the categories list, whether it be cameras, china, old comics or Victoriana. To take part you have to register and get a username and password. There's lots of help for new users, both buying and selling. Some sellers agree to an **escrow** facility where a third party holds the item until the buyer has inspected it. The payment terms, generally postal order, bankers draft or personal cheque, are listed for each item. An increasingly popular way of paying, however, is by e-mail as explained in the next section.

Money by e-mail

If you need to pay for your auction bid or to transfer money to a colleague, but don't wish to send cheques through the post or use a credit card, another way is by e-mail. A popular site is NOCHEX.

  Go to **www.nochex.co.uk**

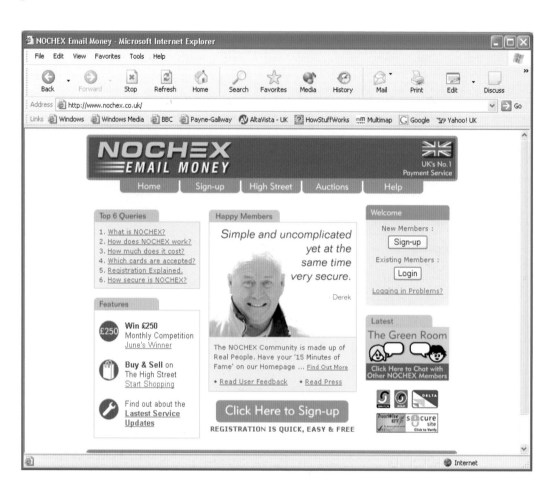

Figure 6.19: NOCHEX

Here you can send money to or receive it from anyone with an e-mail address and a UK debit card. Having opened your NOCHEX account you simply transfer money into it from your bank account or from other NOCHEX users. Similarly you can withdraw money from it into your bank account. You can use it to send money to friends or retailers, or to settle online auction bids. The recipient receives the money instantly and can transfer it to their UK bank account. They don't need to have a NOCHEX account. There is a cost per bank transfer but you don't have the inconvenience and delay of banking a cheque.

Similarly you can request money from anyone with an e-mail address, and they don't need to have a NOCHEX account either.

Travel

a2btravel (www.a2btravel.com) has everything you need: flights, hotels, packages, ferry timetables, autoroute tolls, B&B, villas, skiing holidays, rail and flight schedules.

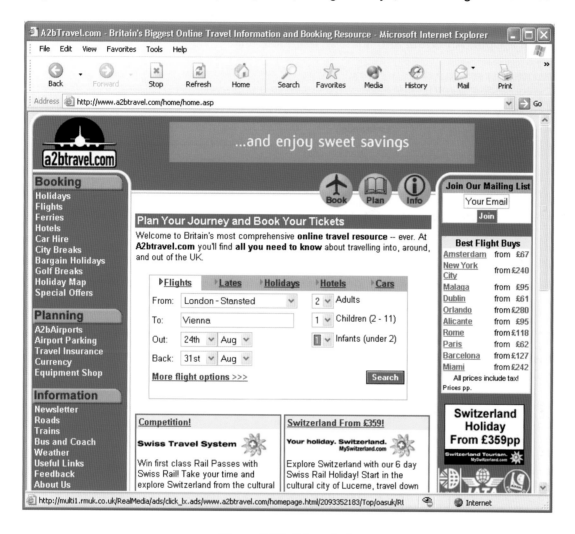

Figure 6.20: A travel site

For cheap package holidays at short notice, visit www.lastminute.com.

Perhaps you haven't decided where to go yet? Have a look at **TimeOut** (www.timeout.com) and **Rough Guides** (www.roughguides.com).

Language translation

While language dictionaries are plentiful there are few sites that can translate whole passages or web sites. One that does – and free – is **Babelfish**, which is part of AltaVista.

 Open **AltaVista** and find the **Translate** link.

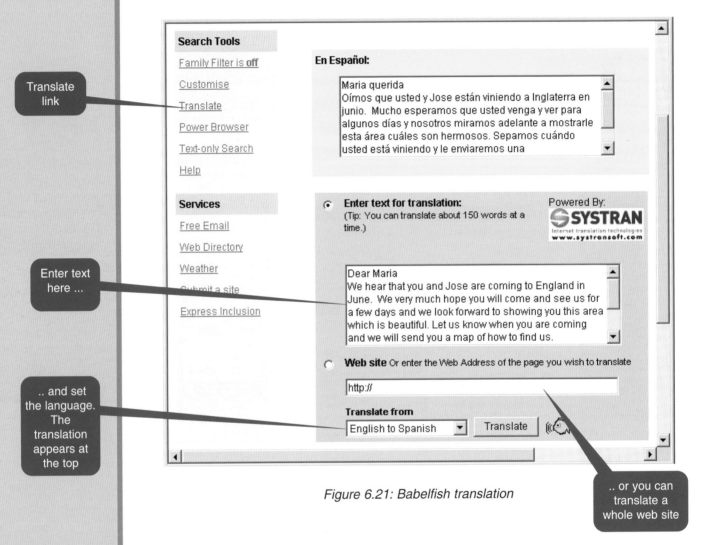

Translate link

Enter text here ...

.. and set the language. The translation appears at the top

.. or you can translate a whole web site

Figure 6.21: Babelfish translation

 Enter the text or web site for translation, set the language and click **Translate**.

Babelfish currently translates to and from French, German, Spanish, Italian, Portuguese, and even Russian, Korean and Japanese! The results may sometimes be curious but (if one avoids idioms like 'out of sight, out of mind'), quite adequate.

Chapter 7
Sending E-mail

E-mail or electronic mail can be sent over the Internet to anybody who has an **e-mail address**. It arrives almost instantaneously anywhere in the world.

To use e-mail, you need both an e-mail address and a program to handle it. Both are available free.

E-mail addresses

E-mail addresses are quite like web site addresses and made up in much the same way. The format is always:

> ## username@domain_name

Here, **username** is you and domain_name is either the **Internet Service Provider (ISP)** who gives access to the Internet, or a web site address.

Sam Brown's personal address might look like any of these:

sam-brown@compuserve.com

sam-brown@aol.com

sam@brownfamily.demon.co.uk

Alternatively, if you have your own registered web site name, your e-mail address can be a part of the site name – oliver@payne-gallway.co.uk for example. This has the advantage that if you switch ISPs your e-mail address remains the same.

An e-mail address has no spaces and is usually all in small letters. It MUST be entered correctly or the message will come back undelivered. Every e-mail address is unique.

Note:
Some ISPs you may have heard of are AOL, Demon, Virgin, CompuServe, HotMail, FreeServe, BTInternet, TescoNet, … and more are popping up all the time.

Using Outlook Express

The program most often used to handle e-mail is **Microsoft Outlook Express** which comes with **Internet Explorer**.

▶ In Windows 98 onwards, click the **Outlook Express** icon near the **Start** button, otherwise select **Start**, **Programs**, **Outlook Express**

Outlook Express

The **Outlook Express** window allows you to:

compose messages

send and receive messages

reply to messages

forward messages

print messages

keep contact names in an **Address** book

file old messages in a folder.

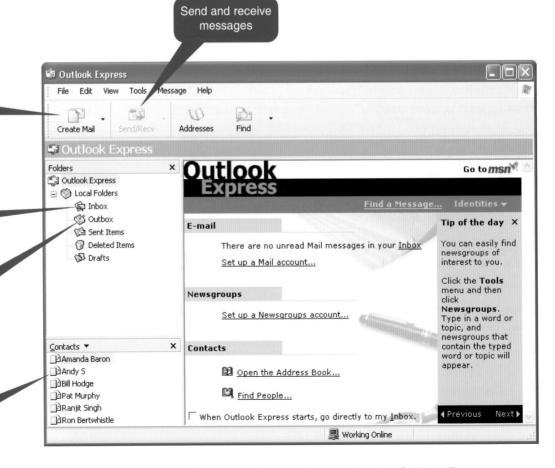

Figure 7.1: Preparing to send or receive e-mail using Outlook Express

Composing an e-mail

To start a new message to someone, you obviously need to know their e-mail address.

▶ Click the **New Mail** button (**Create Mail** in version 6) on the toolbar.

The **New Message** window opens.

▶ Type the address in the **To:** box.

▶ Leave the **Cc:** box blank. This is used if you want to send a copy of the message to someone else.

▶ Type something in the **Subject:** box to say what the message is about.

▶ Type the message in the main window (the message box).

Tip:
Clicking **Send** is like putting a letter in an envelope ready for the post – it's not on its way yet!

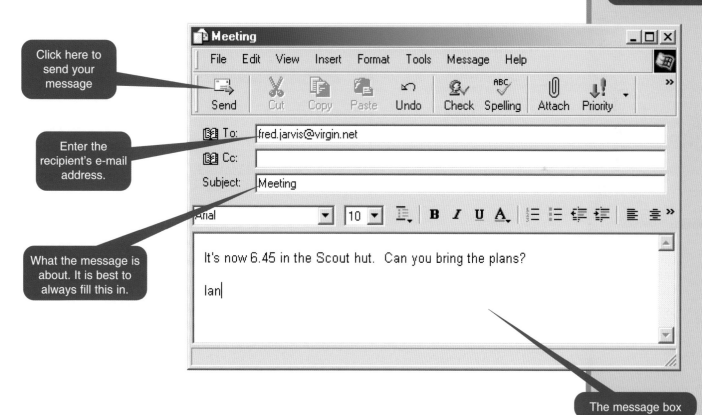

Figure 7.2: Writing a message

▶ Click the **Send** button on the toolbar.

▶ If prompted to **Connect**, click **Cancel**.

The Outbox

The **New Message** window closes and your message is now in the **Outbox**. It has not actually been sent yet – you are still offline. You can write messages to several people and store them in the **Outbox**. When you are ready, you can send them all at once – this uses only a few seconds of online time and saves on the phone bill!

You can look at the contents of the **Outbox** and edit a message before you send it. You can also delete a message if you change your mind about sending it.

To edit a message in the **Outbox**:

▶ Click **Outbox** in the **Folders** pane to select it.

▶ Double-click the message header in the **Message List** pane.

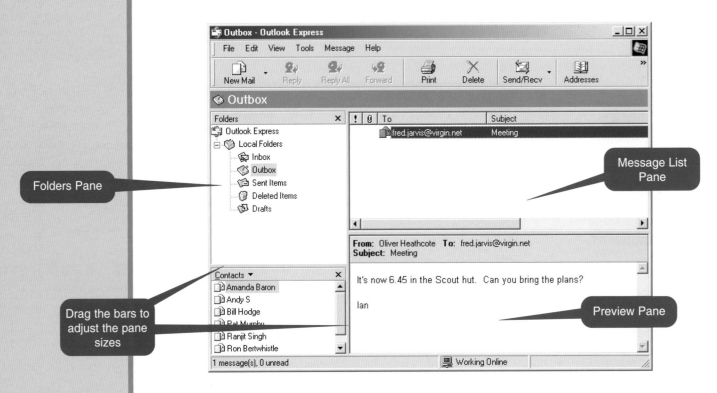

*Figure 7.3: Editing a message in the **Outbox***

An **Edit** window appears and you can edit the message.

▶ Click **Send** to put it back in the **Outbox**.

▶ If prompted to **Connect**, click **Cancel**.

Tip:
Having an **Outbox** means you can write any other messages and send them all at once.

Sending a message from the Outbox

  Click the **Send/Recv** button on the toolbar. ───────

If you are offline, you will be prompted to go online. In this case click **Yes**, then **Connect** at the next prompt.

If the **Hang Up When Finished** box is checked, the **Send and Receive All** option disconnects you automatically as soon as all messages have been sent and any messages for you have been received.

Alternatively, you can send a message as soon as you have written it.

▶ Click the **Send** button.

▶ Click **Connect** when prompted.

The message will be sent straight away. The Outbox is now empty.

The Address Book

The **Address Book** is used to save the addresses of people you regularly send messages to, so that you don't have to type in their address each time.

▶ Click on the **Addresses** button (see Figure 7.1). ───────

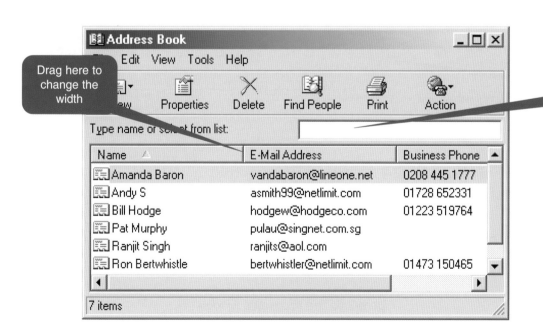

Figure 7.4: The Address Book

Entering a new address

The **Address Book** window lists any contacts who are already entered. To enter a new contact:

▶ Click on the **New** button on the toolbar and choose **New Contact** from the dropdown menu.

The **Properties** window stores the e-mail, home, and other details of each contact.

▶ On the **Name** tab, enter the **First:** and **Last:** names and **Title:**, with **Middle:** and **Nickname:** as well if you like.

▶ Click the arrow on the **Display:** box and choose how you want the name displayed.

▶ Enter an e-mail address.

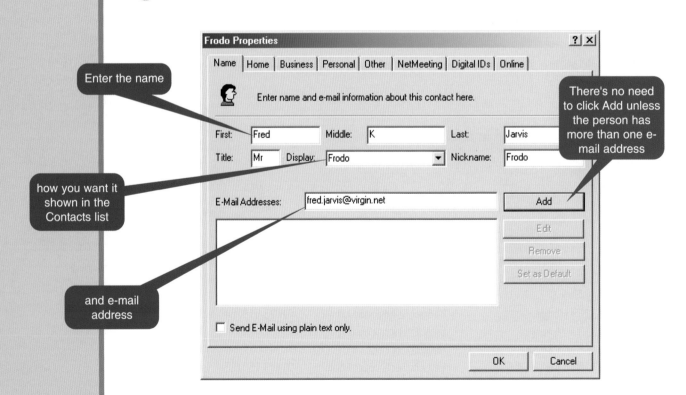

Figure 7.5: The Properties window

▶ Click **OK** to enter the address.

The name is now listed in the **Address Book** window.

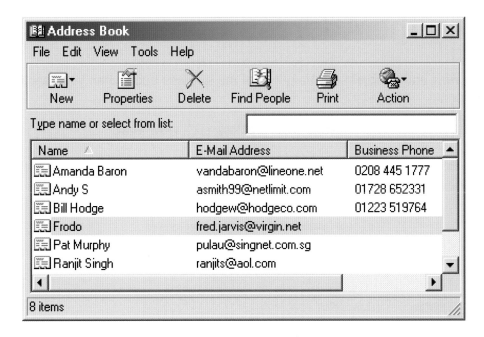

Figure 7.6: Entries in the Address Book

If you need to change it, say to add the home address:

▶ Select the name in the list and click the **Properties** button. ——————————————

▶ On the **Home** tab, enter the details and click **OK**.

> The Properties window lets you keep all sorts of details and is very useful

Jules Properties   **?** **X**

| Summary | Name | Home | Business | Personal | Other | NetMeeting | Digital IDs |

Enter home-related information about this contact here.

Figure 7.7: The Properties window

▶ Now enter two more addresses and close the address book.

Using the Address Book

You can now enter addresses straight from the address book when you send a message.

Note:
Create Mail
in Outlook
Express 6.

▶ In the **Outlook Express** main window, click **New Mail**.

▶ In the New Message window, click on the icon to the left of **To:** (instead of in the box).

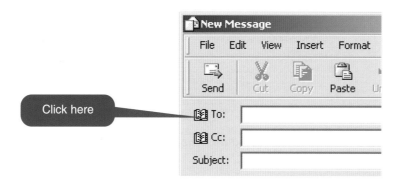

Click here

Figure 7.8: The New Message window

The **Select Recipients** window opens.

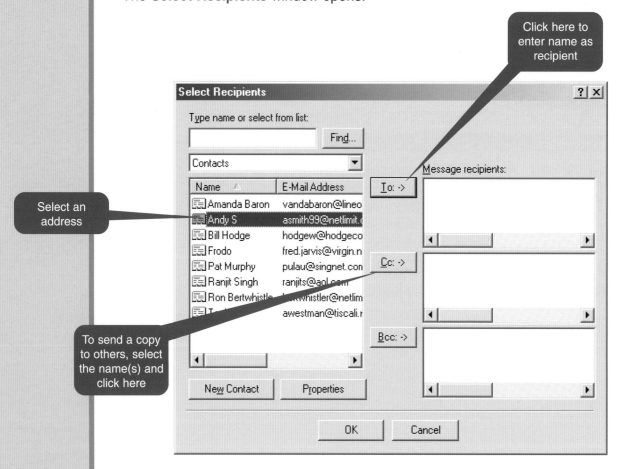

Click here to enter name as recipient

Select an address

To send a copy to others, select the name(s) and click here

Figure 7.9: Selecting an address

Selecting recipients

In the **Select Recipients** window:

 Select an entry in the **Name** list and click on **To: ->** to transfer it to the **Message Recipients** list.

In the same way you can send a copy of your message to someone else just to keep them posted.

 Select another entry in the **Name** list and click on **Cc: ->** to copy it over.

Note: Cc stands for **Carbon copy**. When the recipients read a message, they can all see who else got it too. To send someone a copy without the other recipients knowing, enter their name in the **Bcc: ->** box. (This stands for **Blind carbon copy**).

 Click on **OK** to return to the **New Message** window.

The recipients are all selected now.

Figure 7.10: Ready to type the message

 Type in a subject line and a message.

Formatting a message

You can use the buttons on the **Formatting** toolbar to make text bold, underlined, etc. Notice the formatting options are grayed out until you click in the message area. As soon as you've entered the message you can try them out.

> The **Formatting** toolbar has the usual word processing text options, in addition to the **Cut**, **Copy**, **Paste** and **Undo** functions on the main toolbar.

> Try 36pt Arial bold italic red text!

Figure 7.11: A formatted message

Your message is now complete and ready to send.

> **Note:**
> Although you can format your message using **Outlook Express**, not all recipients will see the formatting. The above message received in **CompuServe**, for example, will look like this:

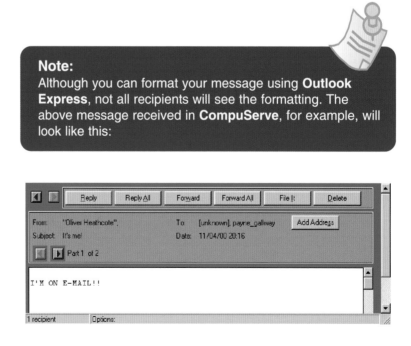

Figure 7.12: Formatting disappears in recipient's message

Chapter 8
Handling E-mail

Sending messages

As you have already seen, you can send a message straight from the **New Message** window but it's much better to send all the messages from the **Outbox** so that in case of trouble they are still there.

 Click the **Send/Recv** button on the toolbar.

If you are offline, you will be prompted to go online: in this case click **Yes**, then **Connect** at the next prompt.

Outlook Express now sends all messages from the **Outbox**, and if there are any messages waiting in your mailbox, it downloads them from the server (a computer belonging to your Internet Service Provider somewhere) to the **Inbox** (somewhere on your hard disk).

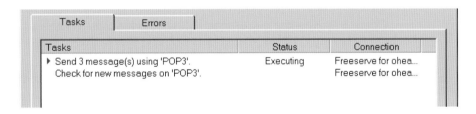

Figure 8.1: A message is displayed telling you what is happening

Warning:
If anything goes wrong while sending from the **New Message** window, you could lose the message and have to type it all in again!

Viewing sent messages

Sometimes it is useful to be able to look up a message you sent last week or last month, to remind yourself what you said. All the messages you send are saved automatically and kept until you delete them.

▶ Click on **Sent Items** in the main window to see what you sent.

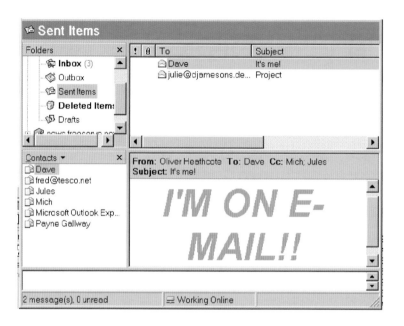

Figure 8.2: Reading a message that you sent earlier

Receiving messages

▶ Click on **Inbox** to show any messages received.

Click here to change the sort order

The number in blue shows how many new (unread) messages you have

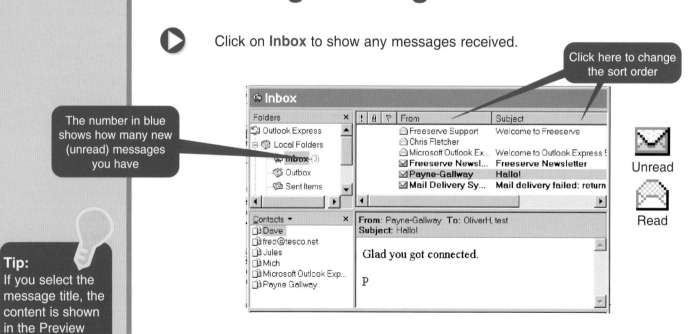

Unread

Read

Tip:
If you select the message title, the content is shown in the Preview pane below.

Figure 8.3: Receiving messages

These are shown on the right with icons indicating **Read** or **Unread**. You can sort the messages by sender, date and so on either by **View**, **Sort By**, or by clicking the column header. The message is shown in the **Preview** pane below but it is easier to view it in a separate window.

 Double-click on the message name in the **Message List** pane.

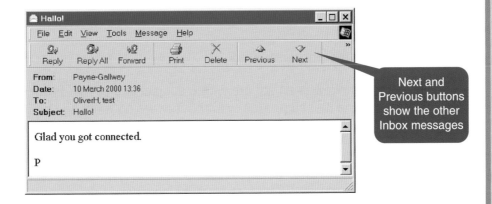

Figure 8.4: Viewing a message in its own window

Note:
If you right-click on the name in this window, or on the message in the message list, you can add the sender to the Address Book.

The **Message View** window lets you:

read and print out the message

write a reply

forward it to someone else

print a message by clicking the **Print** button

Replying to a message

 Click on the **Reply** button on the toolbar.

The reply window is all set up for you to type a reply to the sender only. **Reply All** sends a reply to anyone else that that message was sent to.

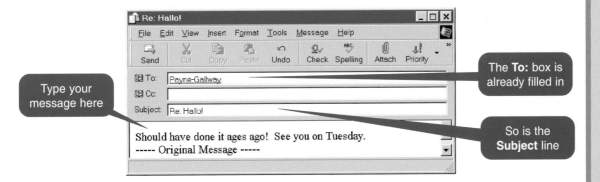

Figure 8.5: Replying to a message

 Type your message and click **Send**.

If you are online it will be sent immediately, otherwise it is put in the Outbox.

Tip:
You can set up Outlook Express to send all messages to the outbox (see page 95).

Forwarding a message

A message sent to you might be of interest to someone else too. Try forwarding a message.

 Double-click on the message name in the **Inbox** to show the message view window.

  Click on the **Forward** button.

The forwarding window is all set up, with a subject line of **Fw: [your message title]**. The cursor is in the message area with the forwarding message below.

 Click **To:** to add the recipient's name.

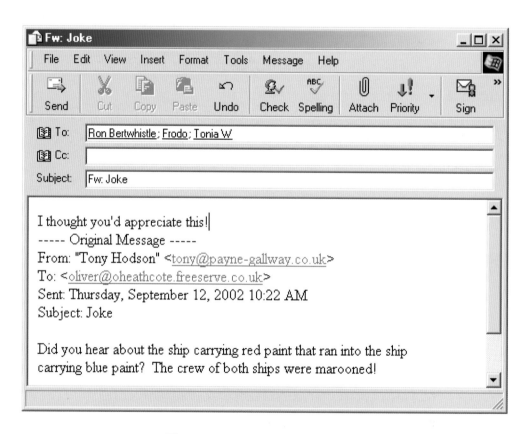

Figure 8.6: Forwarding a message

 Add your own message if you like and click **Send**.

Managing Messages

Once you have sent and received quite a few messages, they start to build up in the **InBox** and **Sent Items**. You need to **delete** those you don't need and **file** those you do. Rather than do this message by message, it's much quicker to select several at once in a list, and then either delete or file them.

Selecting from a list

Suppose you want to select five messages in the **Inbox** list. If these are all together:

 Select the first, then hold down **Shift** and click on the last.

If the messages are not together:

 Select the first, then hold down **Ctrl** and click on each. Notice that this is a **toggle**: if you **Ctrl-click** on a selected message, it deselects it.

Deleting messages

It's best to be ruthless and delete any message you don't need to keep. This includes nearly everything in **Sent Items**. To delete messages:

 Select the messages in the **Sent Items** folder and click the **Delete** button. ——————

Filing messages

You'll probably want to file some messages you have received and delete the others. To file messages:

 Select the messages in the main window.

Figure 8.7: Selecting messages

 From the **Edit** menu, choose **Move to Folder**.

The **Move** window shows all the **Local Folders** you see in the Folders Pane. You need to make a new folder.

 Click the **New Folder** button and type a name for the folder, such as *Personal*.

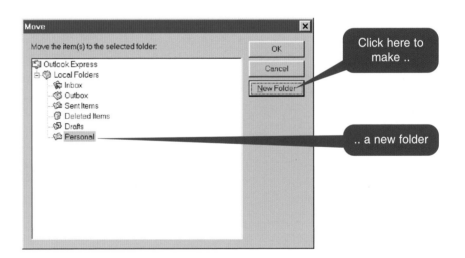

Figure 8.8: Making a new folder

 Click **OK**, then **OK** again to move the messages from the Inbox to your new folder.

If you get interrupted in the middle of writing a long e-mail and aren't sure when you can continue, just click **Send** (don't connect) to put it in the Outbox, then move it to the **Drafts** folder. You can then finish it at leisure and copy it into a new message – you can't move things to the Outbox.

Chapter 9
Attachments

As well as text you can also **attach** a file to the message. For example, you might want to send a scanned photograph of yourself or your family on holiday.

Sending an attachment

To attach a file in the **New Message** window:

▶ Click on the **Attach** button on the toolbar.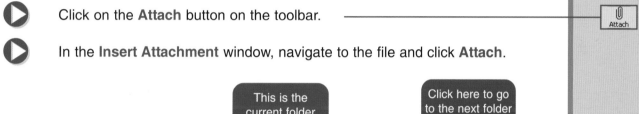

▶ In the **Insert Attachment** window, navigate to the file and click **Attach**.

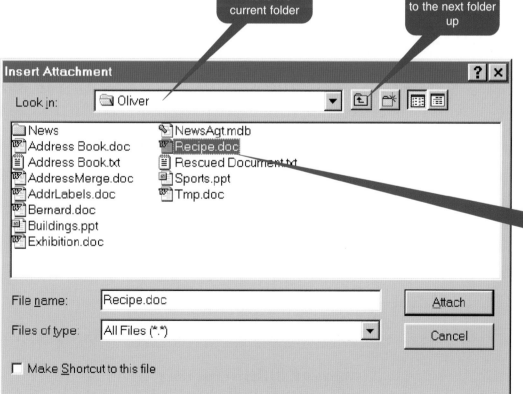

Figure 9.1: Attaching a file to a message

When you send the message, the attached files go too.

Tip:
This could be a word processed document, spreadsheet, graphics file, sound file, game file, etc.

Receiving an attachment

If you receive a file with an attachment, the message header has a paper clip icon beside it.

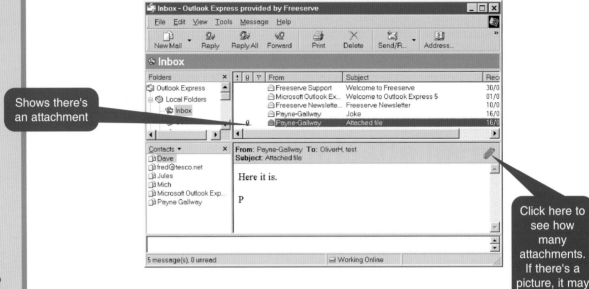

Shows there's an attachment

Click here to see how many attachments. If there's a picture, it may appear in the pane below

Figure 9.2: Receiving an attachment

**Warning:
VIRUS ALERT!**
Make sure you have an up-to-date virus checker installed. It is wise not to open files with **.exe**, **.scr** or **.vbs** extensions unless you are expecting them.

Saving an attachment

You might want to save an attached file to your hard disk if you want to keep it permanently. Otherwise, when you delete the message you'll delete the attachment too.

 Choose **File, Save Attachments**.

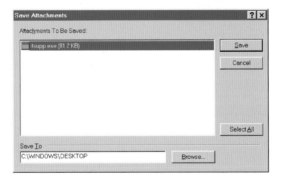

Figure 9.3: Saving an attachment

The default folder for saving attachments is **Windows\Desktop** but you can change this with the **Browse** button.

 Click **Save**.

 Double-click the attached file's icon to open it.

Compressing (zipping) a file

If the total size of the file you are sending is more than half a megabyte (500Kb) then you should compress or **zip** it. It takes about 5 minutes to send 1Mb of data using a fast modem.

Most newer PC's have **WinZip** installed.

▶ Find the file that you want to zip in **Windows Explorer** and right-click on it.

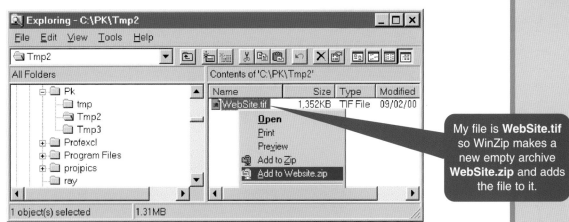

My file is **WebSite.tif** so WinZip makes a new empty archive **WebSite.zip** and adds the file to it.

Figure 9.4: Zipping a file

▶ Choose **Add to *Filename.zip*** from the menu.

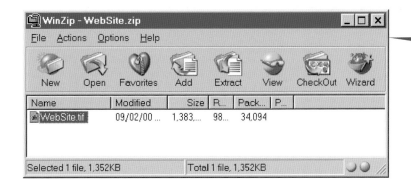

The WinZip window may appear for a moment.

Figure 9.5: The WinZip window

The zip file appears in the same folder.

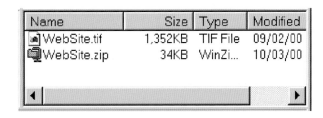

Figure 9.6: The zipped file is much smaller than the unzipped file

Image files, as in this case, are reduced to a fraction of the size.

Unzipping a file

To unzip a zip file:

 Right-click on the file in **Windows Explorer**.

 Choose **Extract to Folder**, and the unzipped file(s) will appear in a subfolder.

Self-extracting files

Although many people have **WinZip**, some do not and it is annoying to download a file you can't do anything with. It is better to make the zip file unzip itself, and this is quite simple.

 Right-click on the **.zip** file in **Windows Explorer**.

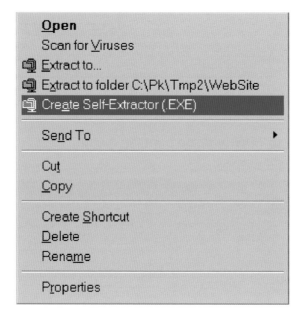

Open
Scan for <u>V</u>iruses
Extract to...
Extract to folder C:\Pk\Tmp2\WebSite
Cre<u>a</u>te Self-Extractor (.EXE)

Se<u>n</u>d To ▶

Cu<u>t</u>
<u>C</u>opy

Create <u>S</u>hortcut
<u>D</u>elete
Rena<u>m</u>e

P<u>r</u>operties

Figure 9.7: Creating a self-extracting zip file

 Choose **Create Self-Extractor (.EXE)** and click on **OK**.

This process creates a file with the same name but ending in **.exe**. This is called an **executable** file: to run it, just double-click on it in **Windows Explorer**, **Browse** to choose the destination folder, then click **Unzip** to unzip the file.

Well, that's it for e-mail … you can now keep in touch with people around the corner or around the world at the touch of a button!

Chapter 10
Going Further

Formatted messages

As well as formatting your message, there is also a choice of patterns and designs to use.

 From the arrow next to the **New Mail** button, choose **Select Stationery** and look at the selection in preview. For example:

Figure 10.1: E-mail stationery

**Reminder:
Create Mail** in Outlook Express V6.

However, formatted messages have to be sent as a separate HTML file which can be inconvenient to receive, so it is generally better to send messages as text only. You can set this for individual contacts in the Address list or for individual messages from **Format**, **Plain Text**. Alternatively use **Tools**, **Options**, **Send**, and set **Mail Sending Format** to **Plain Text**.

Tips and tricks

If you send regular e-mails to a large group – say a newsletter – you can make a **Group** in the Address book (**New** button, **New Group**) and select its members from the address list. Now you just choose the group name as one recipient. When sending a large mailing, each recipient has half a page of addresses at the start of the message, which probably means having to print another page. To avoid this, send the message **To** yourself with the other recipients in **Bcc**.

You may like to add some standard ending to some messages without having to type it all in every time. To do this, go to **Tools**, **Options**, **Signature** and enter the text – or even a scanned image of your signature! You then call it up in the New Message window with **Insert**, **Signature**.

You can back up your address book to a text file using **File**, **Export**. This also works for messages but here it is better to select the folder and choose **File**, **Folder**, **Compact**, which saves the folder as a **.dbx** file.

You can give a message a high **Priority**.

You may want confirmation that a message has been received. In the New Message window you can set **Tools**, **Request Read Receipt** which will e-mail a receipt, but this may not work with some ISPs.

If you have a lot of messages coming in, you can get Outlook to put them in particular folders according to what is in the To:, From: or Subject: lines or the message text using **Tools**, **Message Rules**, **Mail**.

If more than one person in the house uses the same computer, this may cause a logjam of messages and possibly recriminations! By setting up multiple identities and switching between them, each person can have separate messages, contacts and personal settings. **Identities** are set up from the **File** menu.

You can add other e-mail addresses in **Tools**, **Accounts**, **Mail**.

If you don't know someone's e-mail address you can look it up in **People Search** on **Yahoo**.

Help

If you get stuck, try the Help system – choose **Help**, **Contents & Index** or just press the **F1** key.

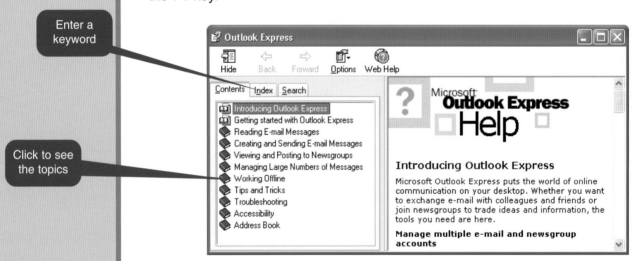

Figure 10.2: Outlook Express Help

Web-based e-mail

Whereas it is usual to keep your e-mail messages on your machine, with some ISPs you access your e-mail from a web site and your messages are kept on the web server. This means you have to be online for longer while you deal with them but the advantage is you can check your mail from any computer anywhere that's on the Internet. This can be particularly useful when travelling. The most popular web-based e-mail is Microsoft's **Hotmail**, and it's very quick to open an account – as well as being free.

  In Internet Explorer, go to **www.hotmail.com**

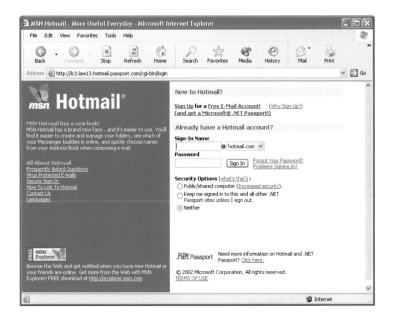

Figure 10.3: Hotmail sign-up

 Click on **Sign up for a free Hotmail Account**

You now enter your preferred e-mail address *yourname*@**hotmail.com** and fill in personal details and a password. The name may already be taken in which case Hotmail will suggest other available possibilities. Write the details down!

 Click **Continue** until your own mailing screen appears.

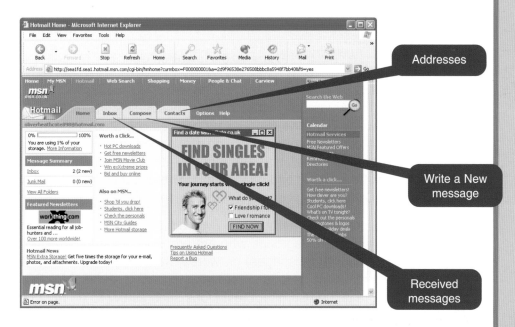

Figure 10.4: Hotmail

This is where you can view your inbox, compose and send a message, add contacts to the address book and manage folders.

 Disconnect when you have finished.

From now on you just sign in. You can also access Hotmail from Outlook Express.

Note:
You'll need to clean out your mail folders occasionally as you are allowed limited space.

Newsgroups

Newsgroups – also called Usenet – are discussion groups sharing ideas by e-mail on every conceivable topic. While the content of many ranges from banal to pornographic, the specialist groups are more serious. You can browse the groups on Google.

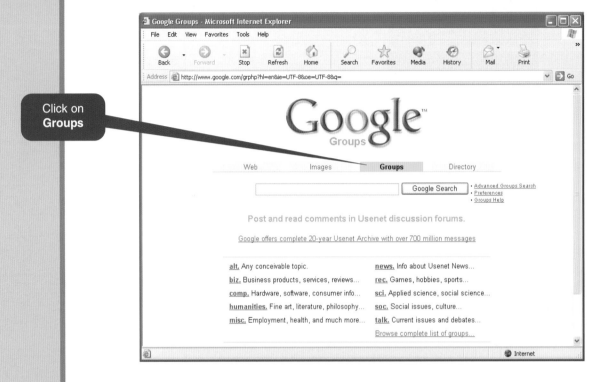

Figure 10.5: Groups on Google

They appear as a list of e-mails and replies which you can follow as a thread. To receive postings from groups is free but you must first subscribe to the ones you want. (See **Outlook Express Help** for further details). Study the conventions of the group before contributing yourself. These groups are not recommended for children – and because of the prevalence of paedophiles on the net often posing as children, they should *never* give any personal details. There is a Newsgroup Connection Wizard on the **Outlook Express** opening screen.

An e-mail etiquette – **netiquette** – has evolved and should be adhered to for fear of arousing the wrath of Newsgroups who are prone to respond by either **spamming** (overwhelming you with messages) or, worse, **flaming** (abusive messages). For example, using all upper-case is regarded as shouting and is BAD FORM. Another part of e-mail lore is the use of abbreviations such as IMHO (in my humble opinion). These save typing but can be over-used and generally say little for the humility of the author's opinion! Similarly, the use of smileys (emoticons) such as :-) is intended to convey mood in the absence of voice. These are also prone to overuse and can be (IMHO) superfluous! For further details on netiquette, see **www.albion.com/netiquette**.

Another resource you can subscribe to is mailing lists – find these on **www.lizst.com**.

Related to Newsgroups is **Internet Relay Chat**, a live discussion on-screen where your messages appear instantly. There are chat rooms on many of the ISP sites and the same anonymity precautions as for Newsgroups should be taken.

Instant Messaging

Instant messaging is a most useful facility both for home and the office and is offered on several sites. With **MSN Messenger** you download and install software from **http://messenger.msn.com**.

Figure 10.6: Downloading MSN Messenger

You then open **Messenger** from a new button on the Internet Explorer toolbar, sign in giving your Hotmail address, and choose which of your friends/colleagues you want to be talking to.

Figure 10.7: Using MSN Messenger

Forums

Forums are serious discussions, often people seeking help or exchanging ideas on everything from pregnancy, cooking, gardening or why their latest software doesn't work. They can be found on **About.com**, ISP sites and manufacturers' sites.

Spam

Spam is the sending of unsolicited e-mails. These may be just to give latest news from a company you bought something from in which case there is usually an option to Unsubscribe. However, they are sometimes sent – in dozens or even hundreds – to annoy. The spammers obtain address lists by dubious means and generate more at random by sticking a list of given names onto a domain name. To sidestep this, you can replace letters with numbers in your address, for example **ol1ver@lineone.net** instead of **oliver@lineone.net**. There may be an Unsubscribe option but since this tells the sender your address is genuine this is not always a help. It is a good idea to open another e-mail address for dealing with web sites you don't trust.

That's it!

We hope this will have given you some idea about the Web and e-mail, and how they can make life easier and more fun. Nothing stays the same for long on the Internet but you will find extra notes, updates, ideas and more web sites on **www.payne-gallway.co.uk/internet-rfts**

Appendix

Here are some notes on getting up and running, and adjusting settings.

Getting connected

Internet access is available only from an Internet Service Provider (ISP). Between you and the ISP come several options.

Most common is a phone connection, requiring a **modem** (**mo**dulator/**dem**odulator) which these days operates at 56k bits per second (kbps), the minimum practical speed for browsing web pages. Much less common but becoming available is a **broadband** connection, mentioned later.

Generally any PC with at least a 486 processor and Windows 95 upwards will be ready to go (Internet Explorer and Outlook Express version 6 need at least Windows 98) but you must have the modem installed and connected to a phone outlet. Your first step is to choose an ISP such as Freeserve, LineOne etc. Many ISPs are either free (apart from the phone bill) or offer unlimited access for a flat fee. Their software does all the installation for you, including Internet Explorer and Outlook Express which are free. There are lots of free CDs on offer in high-street shops and magazines but it's best to avoid ISPs that use their own e-mail software rather than Outlook Express, such as AOL and CompuServe. Consult **Internet Magazine** or **.net** for current recommendations.

  Put the CD in your PC and just follow the instructions for installation.

At some point Windows will restart and you should finish up with an e-mail address and able to browse the web and send an e-mail. In case of trouble, phone the ISP's Help line – they'll soon be able to spot the problem and it's in their interest to get you up and running.

If the modem is unable to dial out, this may be because the dial tone is interrupted to show there's a message waiting – dial 1571 to hear and delete it. Some ISPs will not connect to a number with Caller Line Identification (CLI) withheld. You should disable Call Waiting if you have it, to stop it interrupting your Internet session.

Tip:
It's also worth checking with your phone company for any special deals.

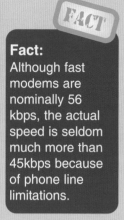
If the connection suddenly stops working, it may be that some settings have been lost. You may be able to spot this by going to **Tools**, **Accounts**, **Mail**, **Properties** which will look something like this:

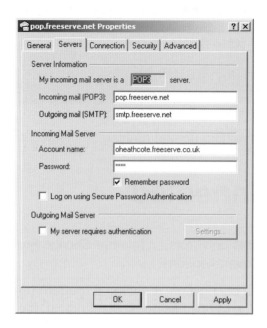

Figure A-1: E-mail account details

There should be entries in all the boxes. Without drowning in acronyms, some that you may meet are:

POP3 – Post Office Protocol version 3; the standard rules that many e-mail clients use to handle incoming e-mail messages.

SMTP – Simple Mail Transfer Protocol; the standard rules that many e-mail clients use to handle outgoing e-mail messages.

HTTP – Hypertext Transfer Protocol; used by web mail such as Hotmail.

IMAP – Internet Message Access Protocol; used by other web mail.

MIME – Multipurpose Internet Mail Extensions; a format for turning an e-mail attachment into text so it can be sent from one e-mail account to another.

If you're feeling confident, you can see your modem settings by looking for **Dial-Up Networking** in Windows Explorer, right-clicking on the connection name and choosing **Properties**.

Broadband connection

Notably this is **ADSL** (Asymmetric Digital Subscriber Line) which is both 10 or more times faster than a standard modem and you can make phone calls at the same time! However, you need to be near an exchange. Another option is via Cable TV. Both of these need a special modem. An **ISDN** (Integrated Services Digital Network) line gives a fast (128kbps) but expensive digital connection requiring a **terminal adaptor** instead of a modem. You can find out more about ADSL from **www.adslguide.org.uk** and about cable options from your local cable company.

With ADSL or cable you are online continuously and it is advisable to install **firewall** software such as **ZoneAlarm** (from **www.zonelabs.com**) to stop anyone hacking into your computer from the outside.

Internet Explorer settings

If the icons on your toolbar don't have names, right-click on the toolbar and choose **Customize**, then **Show text labels** under **Text options**. Also, if you don't have the Status bar at the bottom, select it from the **View** menu.

Most settings are made on the **Internet Options** window (see Figure 1.8), opened from the **Tools** menu. Here, as well as your home page, you set the number of days to keep pages in History: after 4 weeks the pages start to take up a lot of space in the **Windows\Temporary Internet Files** folder. If your computer seems be going slower and to have less and less space on the hard disk for no apparent reason, this is probably because the Temporary Internet files are piling up – click **Delete Files** to clear them and start again.

Many of these files are **cookies** – small files that web sites put on your computer to save your previous settings and preferences for their site and the pages you visited on it, to help the site customise the view for you the next time you visit. These are usually innocent and can only send back information that you provide. Internet Explorer accepts cookies by default but you can have some degree of control over them via the **Security** pane, **Custom Level**. IE 6 offers flexible cookie management; its new privacy dialogue window offering six settings ranging from 'block all' to 'accept all'. Allowing a web site to create a cookie does not give that or any other site access to the rest of your computer, and only the site that created the cookie can read it.

The **Content** pane screens out sites with offensive material by default and you can make lists of approved or barred sites.

If, as you enter an address, the browser tries to complete the address for you instead of showing a list of matching addresses beneath, select the **Advanced** tab and uncheck **Use Inline AutoComplete**.

Outlook Express settings

You change settings using **Tools**, **Options**. You'll soon see what most options do.

On the **General** tab you can uncheck **Send and receive messages at startup** if you like, and on the **Send** tab, uncheck **Send messages immediately** so they go into the Outbox first. You can also set all e-mails to **Plain Text**.

The general window layout can be altered in **View**, **Layout** and you can experiment with this. Some people prefer not to have the preview pane in spite of its convenience. This is because showing a message containing a virus, even in preview, can trigger the virus. (If you have a suspicious message it's best to close the preview pane then delete it.)

Some viruses in e-mailed files (usually with names ending in **.exe .vbs** or **.scr**) can take over your address book and mail themselves to everybody in the list, making you unpopular. Version 6 warns you when an external program is attempting to access your address book. On the **Tools**, **Options**, **Security** menu, OE also uses the IE 'security zones', which prevents certain HTML codes from being executed automatically. The Virus Protection option lets you block attachments if you receive an infected e-mail: the e-mail will not be displayed but OE shows a message.

Tip:
You can change the text size on a page by **View**, **Text Size**, or scroll the mouse wheel while holding **Ctrl**.

Warning:
Selecting a message – and the top one will always be selected when you start up – could tell the sender it has been read even if you haven't seen it.

Tip:
If you can't see full file names in Windows Explorer, choose **Tools, Folder Options, View**, uncheck **Hide File Extensions** and click **Like Current Folder**.

Index